NOTES

ON

Structure and Functions of Human Body and Effects of Yogic Practices on it

Originally Published by :
I. C. YOGIC HEALTH CENTRE

KAIVALYADHAMA
43, Netaji Subhash Road, Mumbai - 400 002.
• **Tele.** : (0091-22) 2281 84 17 • **Fax:** (0091-22) 2281 04 94
• **E-mail :** kaivalya@bom7.vsnl.net.in

NOTES ON
STRUCTURE AND FUNCTIONS OF HUMAN BODY AND EFFECTS OF YOGIC PRACTICES ON IT

OFFICIALLY RECOMMENDED FOR
DIPLOMA IN YOGA EDUCATION - COURSE

PREPARED BY
SHRIKRISHNA, M.B.B.S., Ph.D.

FOR I. C. YOGIC HEALTH CENTRE
KAIVALYADHAMA,

43, NETAJI SUBHASH ROAD,
MUMBAI - 400 002.

PUBLISHED BY
I.C.Y.H.C., KAIVALYADHAMA,
MUMBAI - 400 002.

FIRST PUBLISHED, 30TH APRIL, 1985
FIRST REVISED, 30TH APRIL, 1988
SECOND REVISED, 28TH NOVEMBER, 2012
REPRINTS, 30TH APRIL, 2022

ISBN 81-902803-5-x

PRICE : ₹ 200/-

Printed by :
ACE ENTERPRISES,
137/A, Madhu-Raj Nagar,
C1-6 & 25, Paud Road, Kothrud, Pune - 411 038.
• **Tel. :** +91 94220 89177 • **E-mail :** info@acetanpure.com

PREFACE

These notes are prepared with a view to give concise and at the same time very precise idea regarding the dynamic aspect of the structure and function of the human body, rather than the mere description of its anatomical and physiological features. Selectively only those points are highlighted which would contribute in better understanding of 'HOW' AND 'WHY' the various Yogic practices, affect the human body.

These notes contain also the brief summary of the research work carried out to investigate the effects of various Yogic practices over 50 yrs. at Kaivalyadhama, Lonavla as well as in other centres all over the world.

Although these notes cover a wide area, the presentation is essentially brief and upto the point. We would like to emphasise the fact that these notes cannot replace the lectures and the discussions during which further clarification, elaboration and interrelationship between various concepts could be presented.

We hope the students of Yoga would find these notes very useful for gaining an insight to the whole Yogic discipline.

DR. P. V. KARAMBELKAR
DIRECTOR
I.C.Y.H.C., KAIVALYADHAMA, MUMBAI

30th April, 1985.

PREFACE

I am happy to bring out the notes "Structure & Functions of Human Body, Effect of Yogic Practices on it" as 2nd Reprint with an addition of few figures to explain the subject clearly.

The notes are meant for the students of G. S. College of Yoga basically and students of yoga in general. Dr. Shrikrishna B. Tengshe while in this Institute of Mumbai Branch prepared the original notes but a deep need was felt to get it reprinted. We have added nothing as the need is not felt. We all are grateful to all who have associated to get the reprint done specially Dr. (Mrs.) S. A. Kulkarni, Medical Officer, Mrs. P. L. Mandke, Office Superintendent, and Shri Nitin Tanpure, our Printer. I am sure students of Yoga will be greatly benefited from this book.

O. P. Tiwari
Secretary,
Kaivalyadhama S.M.Y.M. Samiti,
Lonavla

22nd April, 2004

CONTENTS

PART I
YOGIC CONCEPTS OF BODY FUNCTIONS

PART II
MODERN CONCEPTS OF BODY FUNCTIONS

PART III
REVIEW OF EFFECT OF YOGIC PRACTICES ON HUMAN BODY

CONTENTS CONT....

PART IV
GLOSSARY OF THE IMPORTANT WORDS

PART I

YOGIC CONCEPTS OF BODY FUNCTIONS

GENERAL CONSIDERATION

As Yogic practices were evolved over the years with a specific purpose of influencing various psychophysiological functions, it would be worthwhile for us to know how the structure and the function of the human body was viewed by the Yogins, who contributed in this evolution. These ancient concepts seem to have been based more on an empirical approach and therefore have less objectivity, when they are compared to the modern scientific concepts which are based on experimental, analytical and objective approaches.

The Yogins had arrived at these concepts by introspection, in the form of subjective experiences accompanying various Yogic practices like Asanas, Pranayama etc.; which influence different functions of the body. At the same time, they also used the knowledge of anatomy, as recorded in various Ayurvedic texts. A famous treatise on surgical aspects of Ayurveda called 'Sushruta Samhita' mentions specifically that 'the anatomical description given in that work is not only for the practitioners of Ayurveda but is also for the students of Yoga' (vide Sutra sthana III.17).

It is essential to note here, that from the Yogic point of view the body and mind is never considered as made up of two separate entities. They are rather looked upon as one single composite unit. Similarly the structure of the human body and its function also, were never considered as two separate things but were rather treated as the two aspects of the same organism.

The major concepts which can give us the basic idea regarding what is the nature of the human being, its dynamism, and its body structure and function as were understood by the Yogins; are described below. Here we have to keep one thing in mind, that even though some of these concepts resemble the modern concepts in their basic form, they need to be understood on their own merit without trying to look in them the reflection of the modern concepts all the time.

PANCHA KOSHA

The human being is considered to be existing and carrying out its activities simultaneously at five different levels or planes. The term used for these levels is KOSHA, which literally means the cocoon or the sheath. PANCHAKOSHA, therefore, means the five different levels of existence and operation.

The first level is that of the physical body which is made up of and is sustained by, the food (Anna) which we eat. It is, therefore, known as ANNAMAYAKOSHA (Maya = made up of). This Annamayakosha is enlivened by the life force (Prana) which carries out various physiological functions. This level of physiological activities, is known as PRANAMAYAKOSHA. Apart from the vegetative functions there are various subtle functions e.g. that of the mind and intellect. The level of mental (Manas) functioning, responsible for the feeling of emotion, memory etc. is known as MANOMAYAKOSHA while the level of intellect, rationality etc. (Vijnana) is known as VIJNANAMAYAKOSHA. The level of existence which is beyond all these and which has for its basis a pure Blissful (Ananda) consciousness, is known as ANANDAMAYAKOSHA.

A human being, thus exists simultaneously, on the level of physical body, on the level of physiological-vegetative functions, on the level of emotion and memory, on the level of intellect and on the level of pure consciousness. Not only these five levels exist simultaneously but are inter-linked, interdependent and also interpenetrating.

And as far as the awareness of all these Koshas are concerned, we find that most of the time man is aware of only one or two of his Koshas but never all of them together. It is mainly the gross Physical level of Annamayakosha, keeps his field of awareness occupied, along with the external physical environment. The information of the external world brought in by the sensory organs is known as 'exteroception'. On the other hand, the awareness of the sensation of the internal world is known as 'enteroception'. Through the Yogic practices such as

Asanas and Pranayama, one becomes aware of the various internal activities and through the Meditational practices even further, of the subtle mental operations viz. thoughts, memory, emotions etc. We will not be wrong if we say that the whole of the Yogic discipline aims at increasing the internal awareness, which ultimately embraces the whole of the operational existence of the human being, from the level of gross body to the level of pure consciousness.

This all-embracing new awareness leads to the correct understanding of one's own nature. It is an essential step for gaining a total control over the activities in all the spheres and at all the levels of one's existence. It ultimately culminates in making the personality totally integrated and balanced, denoted by the term SAMADHI.

PRANA

The human body is enlivened by the vital force known as PRANA. This Pranashakti is responsible for the various functions being carried out within the body. There are five basic functions for which this Pranashakti works through its five different aspects. Each aspect is known by specific Sanskrit term, which etymologically denotes its meaning. In the body, particular aspect of the Pranashakti is felt to be more active in some specific area, and accordingly is described to be responsible for the activities of the organs situated in that area.

THE FIVE MAJOR ASPECTS OF PRANASHAKTI

A. PRANA : It is essential for the life activity to go on ceaselessly to replenish the exhausted energy, continuously. The energy is required to be brought in from outside the body either in the form of Oxygen, nutrients or water. The vital force responsible for bringing in the energy in this way, is known as PRANA and its area of activity is from the nose to the chest.

B. SAMANA : After having brought in, the energy source, it needs to be converted into a suitable form, so that the body can use it. This is a process of digestion. The vital force which controls the activity of digestion, is situated in the abdomen above the level of umbilicus and is known as SAMANA.

C. VYANA : After making the energy available in an usable form it has to be transported to each and every part of the human body. This transportation and circulation of energy all over the body is under charge of VYANA and its area of activity covers the whole body.

D. APANA : In the process of continuous utilization of the energy required for various activities, a lot of waste matter is produced. The vital force responsible for expelling unwanted waste matter out of the body is know as APANA, and its area of activity is within the abdomen below the level of umbilicus. It is also responsible for the expulsion of breath.

E. UDANA : Apart from the vegetative functions there is a continuous effort in the body-mind complex to excel itself through the subtle level of functioning which includes expression and communication and the vital force responsible for this activity is known as UDANA. Its area of activity is the head and the neck.

There are also other minor activities carried out by the PRANASHAKTI and these subdivisions of Prana are known by different names according to their function. They are ....

A 'NAGA' for regurgitation
B 'KURMA' for blinking
C 'KRIKAL' for sneezing
D 'DEVADATTA' for drowsiness
E 'DHANANJAYA' for thirst

RELATION OF PRANA AND MANAS :

Pranashakti is responsible for the vegetative functions, but at the same time it steers the subtler psychological functions, too. In Yogic view, therefore, the nature of Prana and Manas (mind) is considered as inseparable. This concept is not much different from the present psychosomatic concepts. We can say that rather it goes one step further as it is repeatedly mentioned in the texts of Hathayoga that one who controls Prana can control the mind and vice versa. Therefore, the practices which try to affect Pranic or the vegetative-physiological activities are obviously considered to affect the mind as well. It is also advocated for the same purpose, that while practising Pranayama the mind should be applied completely to the practice itself thus making the internal awareness as an integral and obligatory part of the Pranayamic practice.

KUNDALINI

KUNDALINI :

There is another psycho-physiological concept in Yoga which is very important. According to this concept there is a higher and potentially very dynamic aspect, to this Pranashakti, which in normal circumstances is never called into action. This aspect remains in the dormant state, symbolically represented by the coiled body of the asleep serpent known as 'kundalini'. Through the yogic practices when it is stimulated, it is awakened and reaches to its highest possible potential. This is compared to the serpent being awakened, which raises itself high, straightening its body and spreading its hood. This rising of the spiritual force is known as the KUNDALINI PRABODHAN i.e. awakening of the serpent power. This brings about the radical change in the person's understanding of the world within and without, known as spiritual enlightenment accompanied by significant psycho-physiological changes.

NADI

The Pranashakti which works all over the body, uses some specific channels through which it moves. These channels or passages are known as Nadis. According to the ancient scriptures there is not a single part in the human body which has not been contacted by anyone of these Nadis. In one of the Hatha Yoga texts it is mentioned that there are three hundred fifty thousand Nadis in the body reaching each and every part of the body. Amongst them three are the most important ones.

A. IDA

This nadi starts on the left side of the base of the spine and while traversing in a spiral way reaches the left nostril. Ida is primarily responsible for all those activities which are anabolic or constructive in nature, which conserve energy and give a cooling effect to the body. It is also symbolically denoted as a female aspect of the energy with a blue colour and is represented by moon as its symbol.

B. PINGALA

This nadi arises from the right side of the base of the spine and while traversing spirally reaches the right nostril. It is responsible for all those activities which are catabolic, destructive or energy consuming in nature and which generate heat in the body. It is symbolically denoted as a male aspect of the energy with a red colour and is represented by the sun as its symbol.

C. SUSHUMNA

This nadi starts from the base of the spine and traverses straight up along the spinal column, up to the opening in the base of the skull, reaching the brain. It is represented by white colour with the fire as its symbol. In normal circumstances Prana is not able to operate through this Nadi. When through the Yogic procedures Sushumna is made functional and the Prana is made to enter it and is allowed to reach the highest centre in the head, it is known as rising of the serpent power or KUNDALINI.

In the Yogic literature we find quite divergent opinions regarding the exact course of these Nadis. Some authorities consider that these Nadis rise from the lower most end of the spine, while some other give the location of their origin as the area just behind the navel region. Even though it is hazardous to look for clear cut anatomical features in these description of the essentially experiential things, we can definitely surmise that at least to some extent these inner experiences are associated with some specific course which concurs with the anatomical features at numerous points.

CHAKRA

Along the course of Sushumna there are six nodal points or centres, through which the Ida and Pingala criss-cross each other in a spiral way. Each of these centres is responsible for the different levels of consciousness as well as for the control of various internal organs. On the arousal of Kundalini, when the Prana starts rising through each of these centres, the energy field in each centre gets activated, thereby influencing the internal functions and evoking the specific levels of consciousness associated with it. In these centres, is represented the concept of hierarchy in the evolution of higher functions, as the grosser functions are represented in the lower centres while more refined one are represented in higher centres. When Prana reaches the highest point in the brain (Sahasrara) consciousness gets altered completely taking the person into transcendental stage known as Turia.

These centres are known as CHAKRAS and their locations along the Sushumna are . . . .

A. MOOLADHARA CHAKRA

This is the lower most Chakra situated at the tail end of the spine, at the level of perineum which is between genital opening in the front and the anal opening behind.

Kundalini lies in its dormant state in this Chakra before being stimulated. In this Chakra four kinds of subtle energies work and therefore it is also represented as a lotus with four petals.

B. SWADHISTHANA CHAKRA

This is situated at the level of pubic symphysis, a bone just above the genital organ. This is the second Chakra in ascending order and is represented as a lotus with six petals because six subtle energies work here.

C. MANIPURA CHAKRA

This is the third Chakra from below and is situated at the level of umbilicus. This is represented as a lotus at the level of umbilicus. This is represented as a lotus with ten petals and the number of subtle energies working here, is ten.

D. ANAHAT CHAKRA

This is the fourth Chakra from below and is situated in the chest at the level of heart. This is represented as a lotus with twelve petals having twelve subtle energies working at this level.

E. VISHUDDHA CHAKRA

This is the fifth Chakra in the ascending order and is situated in the throat. It is represented as the lotus with sixteen petals as sixteen subtle energies work here.

F. AJNA CHAKRA

This is the sixth Chakra in the ascending order which is situated at the level of Bhrumadhya (midbrow). It is represented as a lotus with two petals as two subtle energies operate at this level.

G. SAHASRARA CHAKRA

This is the highest centre in the brain and on reaching here Pranashakti alters the consciousness completely leading to the experience which transcends the time and space limit.

It is essential to keep in mind that these centres though described as Chakras (wheels) or Padma (Lotuses), it is but a symbolic description. These are the energy centres along the Sushumna and as Kundalini ascends through it they get stimulated one by one giving rise to a variety of subjective experiences. This is known as CHAKRA-BHEDANA and the result of this process is the experience of the transcendental state.

PART II

MODERN CONCEPTS OF BODY FUNCTIONS

GENERAL CONSIDERATION

The modern view regarding the structure and function of the body is more objective and more analytical in nature. More important is the insight, which it offers, in the dynamic aspect of the varied forms of the living beings and their activities.

MAIN CHARACTERISTICS OF LIFE-ACTIVITIES :

All the activities of the living beings are basically motivated for the preservation of the self and the preservation of the species. All these activities can be classified under the three major heads.

1. CHANGE IN LOCATION AND SIZE

For the preservation of one's self, perception of changes in one's environment and adaptation to it is a must. For this purpose each organism shows constant change, either in its location i.e. it can move from one place to another towards the food or away from the danger, or shows change in its shape and size in the form of growth, repair and decay.

2. MAINTENANCE OF NUTRITIONAL STATUS

During its activities the organism consumes the energy which requires to be replenished again and again. At the same time lot of things are produced inside the organisms as a consequences of these activities and these being harmful, require to be thrown out of the body. Thus the living organism has to, constantly, keep its internal environment safe for its proper functioning, either by replenishing the consumed energy through respiration, digestion and absorption or expelling the harmful by-products of energy utilisation through excretion.

3. REPRODUCTION

Each living being continuously seeks the propagation of its own form of life through duplicating or reproducing itself. In human beings the story of life becomes a fascinating one. The father's sperm and the mother's ovum which in itself is alive, come together to form a new independent life in the form of fertilized ovum in the mother's womb. This single cell goes on multiplying and after around 45 multiplication stages, forms itself into a mass of hundred million cells. The single original cell in its multiplication gets converted into more and more specialised form; some become very hard like that of bones; some get elongated as long as one meter in length like that of nerve cell; some become transparent like that of the cornea while some others become mobile like that of blood cells. But through all this multiplicity and myriads of functioning there is always a unity. Human body shows a remarkable organisational unity which helps in carrying out all its activities in a co-ordinated and integrated manner. ORGANISATION is the hall-mark of the human body.

For the specific function there are different types of CELLS, evolved specially to carry out that function. These cells when form separate specialised group, it is known as TISSUE. Different tissues come together to form various ORGANS, and different organs come together to form various SYSTEMS of the body. The functioning of all these systems collectively contribute in what is called as BODY FUNCTION. Thus it is essential to realise that the body function is ultimately a collective function of each and every cell which constitutes the body. The proper functioning of each individual cell, therefore, is the most important factor for the survival of the body as a whole.

The cell can function properly provided its environment is favourable. This environment around the cell inside the body is known as the INTERNAL ENVIRONMENT compared to the environment outside the body which is the EXTERNAL ENVIRONMENT. The mechanism through which this INTERNAL ENVIRONMENT is kept constant is known as the process of HOMOEOSTASIS. Through this process, the internal environment of the body is maintained at the relatively constant level. Any derangement in this mechanism is sure to bring a great disturbance in the cellular function and in extreme situation it may even lead to death of the cell.

The structure and the function of the body is intimately linked with each other. The difference between the structure and the function is basically a question of - what changes slower and what changes faster. The structure is relatively more defined and is more durable but none the less it also shows the change along the passage of time. On the other hand the function is more elusive and goes on showing the constant fluctuation. During the growth or decay as the structure changes, function do change, similarly in some conditions change in the function can cause the change in the structure as well. This dynamic inter-relationship between structure and function is a very important factor in understanding the nature of living organism.

All the above general features of the structure and function are shared by the human beings with rest of the animated world. But they have one more feature which distinguishes them from the others. It is the ability to be conscious of one's own consciousness. This SELF-CONSCIOUSNESS forms the basis of the whole endeavour which human beings alone, are capable of undertaking. This is the single most important factor which can influence whole of the human activities. This increases enormously the complexity in the nature of human being.

SYSTEMS OF THE HUMAN BODY :

After having considered the general features of the structure and function, the study of the dynamic aspect of each of the body systems would be essential for understanding the working of the human body. All in all nine specific body systems contribute in keeping the body, active and alive. The Skeletal system and the Muscular system are the principal systems responsible for the movement. The Nervous system and Endocrine system are principally involved in the organisation and control of the whole body. Respiratory system and Cardio-vascular system are responsible for making the Oxygen and nutrients available for the whole body. Digestive and Excretory systems are responsible for making the nutrients available for the body as well as for expelling out the unwanted waste matter from the body.

Ultimately the Reproductive system concerns itself with the propagation of the species. Without going into much finer details, we will try to understand only the essential aspect of the each system.

SKELETAL SYSTEM

The Skeletal system includes all the bones and the joints in our body. This system serves four main functions.

FUNCTIONS OF THE SKELETAL SYSTEM:

1. SUPPORT

It provides a support and gives a firmness to the body.

2. PROTECTION

It protects the various delicate organs like brain and lungs.

3. MOVEMENT

It provides surface for the attachment of muscles and itself acts as lever. Thus along with the muscular system it helps in the movement of various parts of the body or of the body as a whole.

4. BLOOD FORMATION

Within the soft tissue inside the bone known as bone-marrow, blood cells are produced. In the adults it is found in few bones but in newborn and in children it occurs in large number of bones.

BONES :

The live bone is a hard structure but at the same time it also has an elasticity. The hardness is basically because of the deposition of the calcium salt in its matrix and this process of deposition is known as CALCIFICATION. The live bone remains in flux, continuously being formed and broken down. The calcium is continuously released in the blood, whenever the blood level of the calcium goes down. Thus

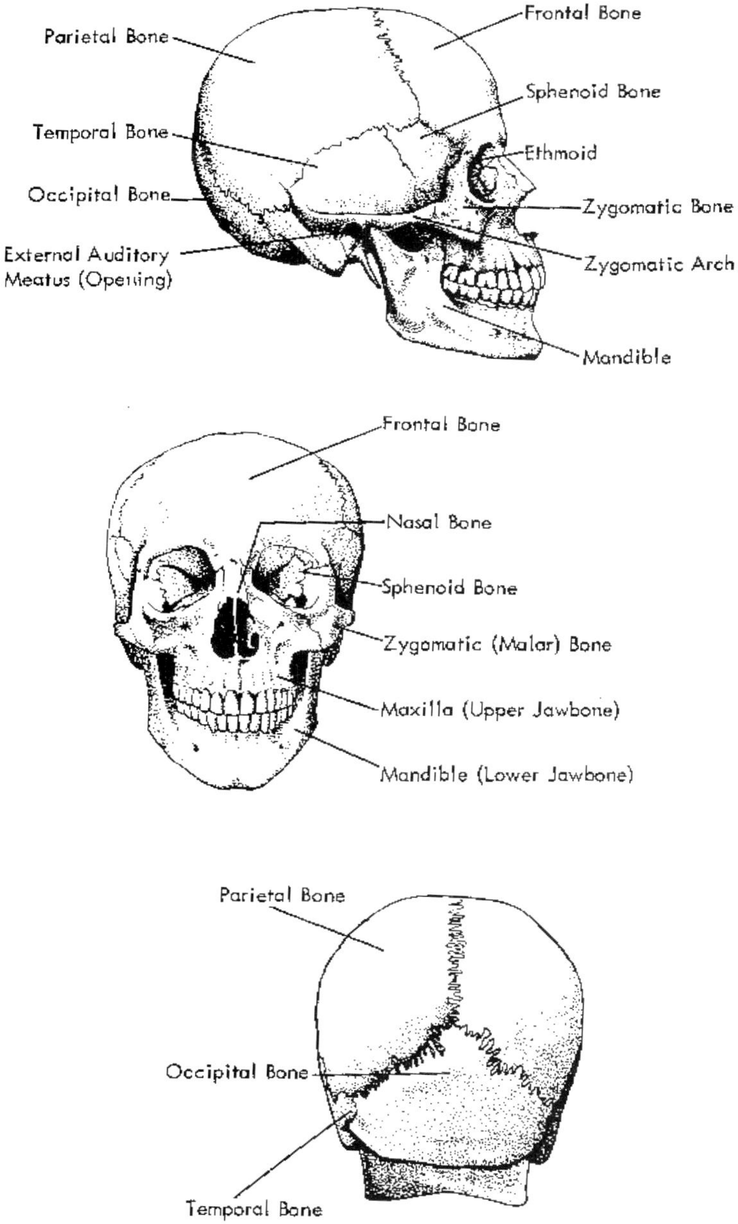

Fig. 1 The Skull

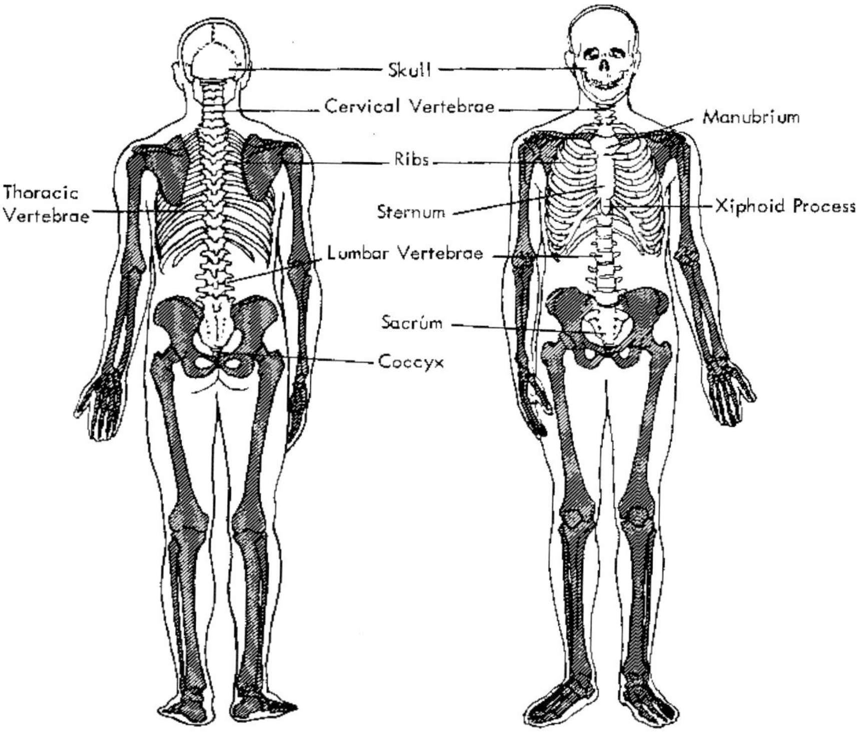

Fig. 2 The Axial Skeleton (Unshaded Areas)

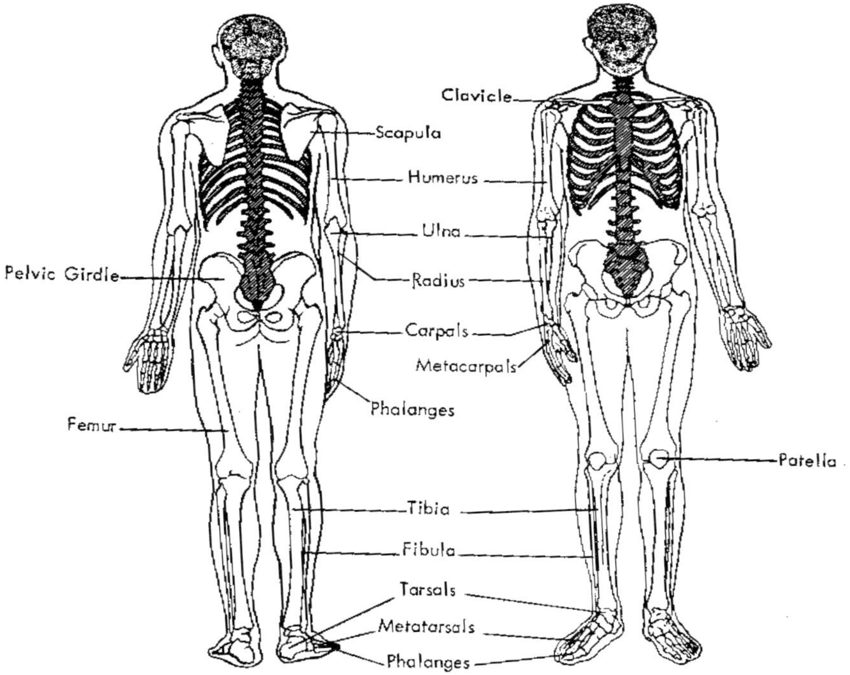

Fig. 3 The Appendicular Skeleton (Unshaded Areas)

the level of calcium and its ratio to other elements like phosphorus in the blood is an important factor in the formation and maintenance of the bone. The factors which are responsible for degeneration of the bones are (1) disturbed proportion of calcium and Phosphorus in the blood, (2) disturbance in the level of hormones like oestrogen, calcitonin and other para-thyroid hormones, and (3) lack of exercise.

Degeneration of the bone causing reduction in the density of the bone is known as OSTEOPOROSIS. Decreased activity leading to a reduction in the normal stress and strain placed on the bone is a major factor in the development of osteoporosis. Weight bearing and muscle pull over the bony surface helps in maintenance of the normal density of the bone. Exercise that alters the amount of weight on each foot, attempts to balance on one foot, involves raising the heel off the floor etc. helps in maintenance of the bone in healthy condition.

JOINTS :

When the two bones come together to form the joint, they form the most vital part of the Skeletal system. In infants, all the joints remain moveable. But as the child grows, some of the joints fuse together to give the additional rigidity to various parts e.g. skull. The opposing surfaces of the moveable joints are usually covered by the smooth but firm carilegenous tissue which reduces the friction to the minimum and at the same time allows weight bearing without any discomfort. These joints are held in position firmly by the ligaments attached to the bones all around the joint surface. Some times there are also ligaments inside the joints to give a further firmness. All these joints are lined internally by Synovial membrane which secretes the oily synovial fluid. This fluid acts as a lubricant and allows the surfaces to move easily over one another. The integrity and the proper functioning of the joint depends on the health of three factors : cartilage, ligaments and synovial membrane. Disturbance in any of these, is sure to lead to the restriction of the function of that joint, as can be seen in the condition of osteo-arthritis, Rheumatic arthritis or in case of recurrent dislocation of shoulder joint etc.

THE SPINE :

The spine or the Vertebral column forms one of the most important part of the Skeletal system. It is an amazing piece of nature's work. It is at the same time an organ of stability and mobility, of support and protection, of resistance and adaptation. It is an instrument of great precision yet of robust structure.

In adults it is formed of 24 moveable parts known as vertebrae and the two lower most fused parts known as sacrum and coccyx. Each vertebra forms a joint with upper as well as the lower vertebra and is held in position by the ligaments which runs from the top to the base of the spine.

At birth the whole of the spine has only a forward curve known as primary curvature of the spine. When the child learns to lift its head, a backward curve is added to the spine in the neck region and as the child learns to stand upright, one more backward curve is added in the lumbar region. These are known as secondary curvatures of the spine. Thus in the adult, the shape of the spine is like that of an extended spring with two backward curves : one in the cervical and the other in the lumbar region and two forward curves : one in thoracic and the other in the sacral region. These natural curves help in two ways : (1) it counter-balances the forward and downward pull of the various organs attached to the front part of the spine inside the thorax and the abdomen, (2) it also helps in the absorption of the shock during the movement in upright standing condition and while walking.

These natural curves of the spine can get disturbed either by disappearance of these curves when the spine becomes flat or by increase in the forward curve : mainly in the thoracic region (with convexity backward) known as KYPHOSIS or by the exaggeration of the backward curve mainly in the lumber region (with convexity forward) known as LORDOSIS. It can also get disturbed by the addition of sideway curves known as SCOLIOSIS. When the natural curves in the spine are thus altered, it leads to various functional disturbances. Not only can the lungs not expand fully and the intestine

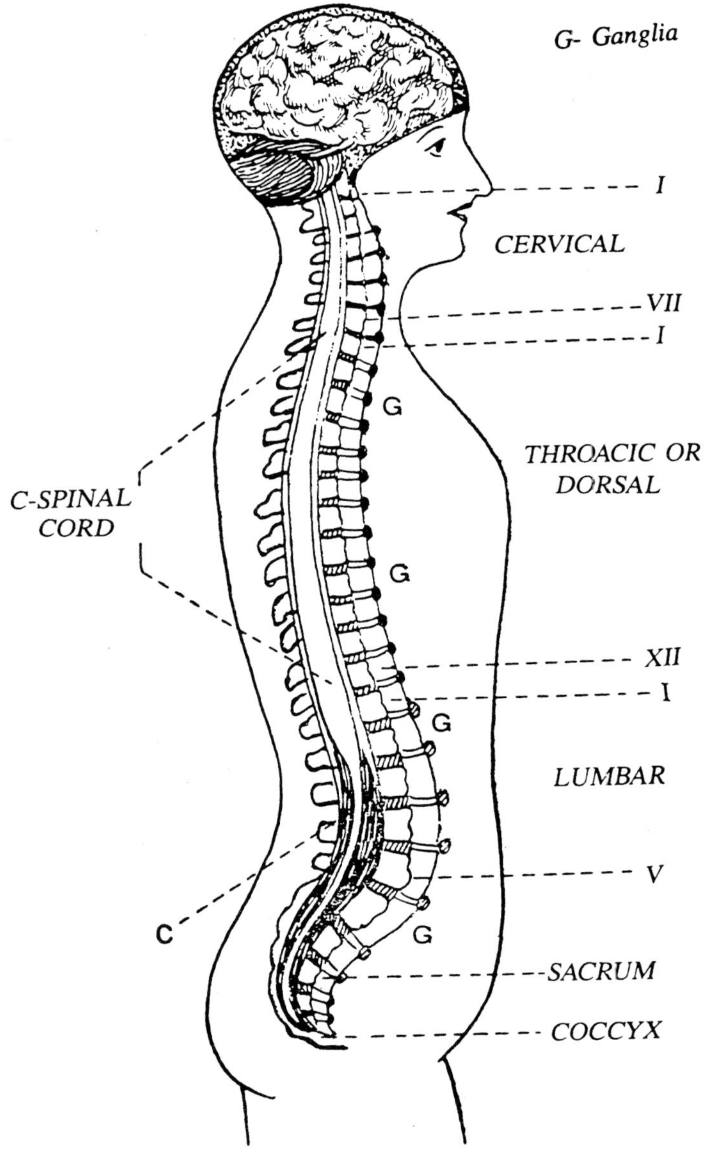

Fig. 4 The Vertebral Column, the Brain, the Spinal Cord and the Sympathetic Ganglia

function properly but also the muscles have to work under strain as the posture of the whole body gets disturbed by these alteration in natural curves. The disturbance in the alignment of the vertebral column can also lead to an unhealthy pressure over the peripheral nerves as they emerge out through the intervertebral foramina, causing para-aesthesia (change in the feeling of different sensations) and even the paralysis of the muscles in the extreme cases.

MUSCULAR SYSTEM

Muscular tissue is specialized for contraction and is therefore able to produce movement. Wherever there is movement in the body, there must be muscular tissue to produce it. Muscle cells are called muscle fibres because of their shape.

Each muscle is a bundle of lengthwise small thread like fibres known as MYOFIBRILS. Each of myofibrils has three main qualities; it can contract and shorten its length when stimulated. It can get elongated whenever required and it has the elasticity to come back to its original shape when no action is called for. This contractibility, extendibility and elasticity endow the muscles its unique function.

There are three types of muscular tissue : Voluntary, involuntary and cardiac. Muscles attached to bones, responsible for the locomotion and under the control of will power are skeletal, somatic, voluntary or striated muscles. On the other hand the muscles which go into the formation of various visceral organs and function autonomously are known as visceral, involuntary or smooth muscles. The muscles found in the heart are of special variety and are known as Cardiac muscles.

MUSCLES IN GENERAL SERVE FOLLOWING FUNCTIONS

1 MOVEMENT

Along with the skeletal system the skeletal muscles bear the responsibility for the locomotion and as a part of the visceral organ, the visceral muscles bear the responsibility for the various internal

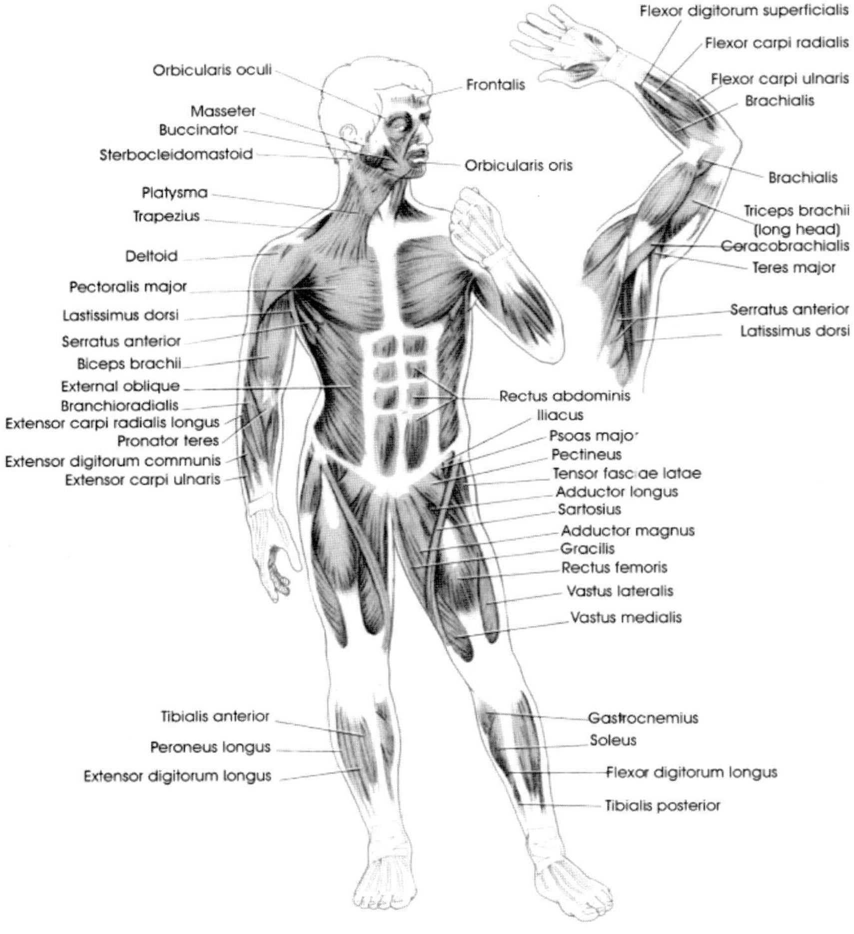

Fig. 5 Principal Superficial Muscles (a) Anterior View

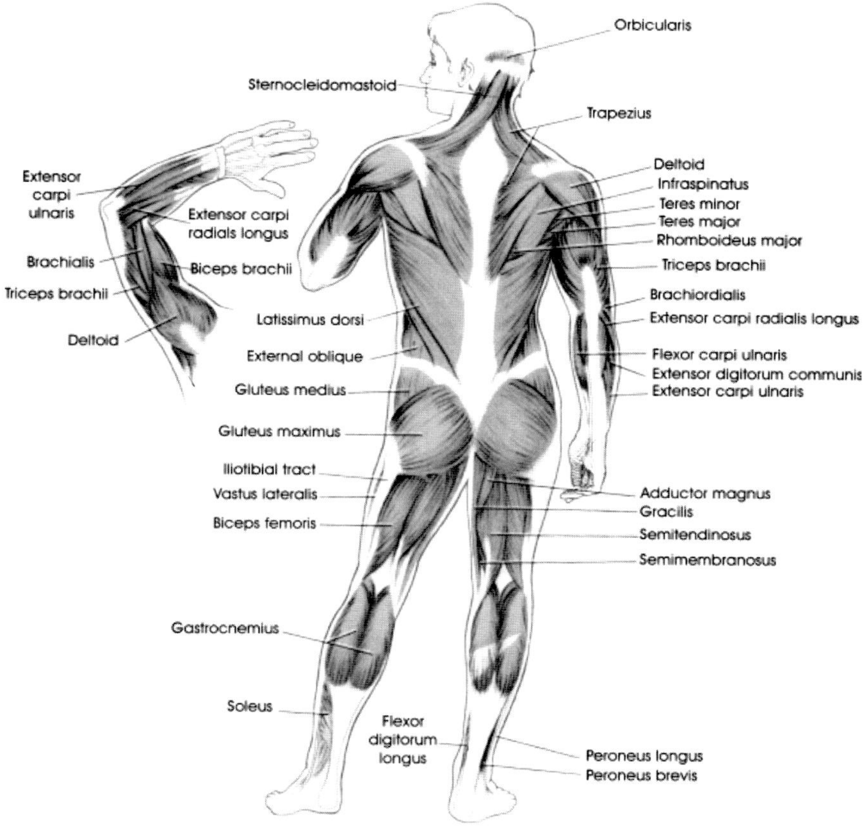

Fig. 6 Principal Superficial Muscles (b) Posterior View

dynamic actions, like pumping of the heart, propulsion of the food in the intestine, resistance to and diversion of blood flow by constriction and dilation of the blood vessels etc.

2 PROTECTION

Skeletal muscles contribute in the formation of the chest cage and gives the protection to the lungs, and by forming the strong sheet in front of the abdominal cavity, protects the intra-abdominal organs. Thus it acts as one of the important protective mechanism of the body.

3 CLOSURE OF THE VARIOUS OPENINGS

By forming the strong sphincters around the openings it controls the entry and exit along the various passages e.g. anal sphincters around the anal opening or the cardiac and the pyloric sphincters around the proximal and distant end of the stomach.

4 HEAT PRODUCTION

The SKELETAL muscles have a major share in the production of body heat and play an important part in the homoeostasis of the temperature.

5 VENOUS RETURN

The skeletal muscles of the lower extremity by their continuous contraction and relaxation squeeze and release the veins running through them, making the blood flow upward against the gravity. The valves inside the veins which open upward alone, help in dividing the blood column into smaller parts and make it easy for the muscles to squeeze the blood upward by contracting around the vein. Thus muscles have the important role in the return of the blood, towards the heart against the gravity. Thus it prevents the pooling of the blood in the lower extremity.

6 MAINTENANCE OF POSTURE

The continued partial contraction of different skeletal muscles makes possible: standing, sitting and other maintained positions of the body.

POSTURE :

Posture is defined as the position or the alignment of the body parts. It is called a good posture when it favours the function. When the posture is good there is no undue strain over the muscle to maintain it. The energy requirement for the maintenance is minimum and it contributes to the minimum of fatigue. There is no undue strain over the muscles and bones and it interferes least in the functioning of Cardio-Respiratory, Digestive-Excretory systems. Any bad posture on the other hand makes the fatigue set in easily, and disturbs the various functions of the body. The posture is also intimately linked to the mental attitude.

MUSCLE ACTION :

Voluntary muscles are masses of striated or skeletal muscle fibres aligned, so that their contractions, though individually small force, collectively provide much power. Not all fibres in a muscle contract at any one time, though large numbers do when necessary; pull is varied by changing the number of fibres contracting at one time. Groups of fibres, they become fatigued, are replaced by others, which have been resting.

During the routine movement muscles act in a group. When the muscle contracts the power of contraction depends on the number of muscle fibres contracting simultaneously. In the routine movement more than one muscle contracts at a time. The group of muscles which contract simultaneously and are responsible for the action ensued thereby are known as PRIME MOVERS.

At the same time when the muscles on the opposite side relax or allow to get stretched so that the prime movers can contract, they are known as Antagonists. When other group of muscles contract to help the prime movers by assisting in the movement of the prime movers, they are known Synergists and when they contract simultaneously with the prime movers to hold the body parts rigid as in the case of stabilization of knee joint while standing they are known as Fixators.

In the normal circumstances there is always a continual partial contraction of the few of the muscle fibres which gives a tautness rather than causing the recognised contraction of the muscle leading to the movement. This partial contraction in the various muscle fibres occurs in relay, giving the continuous minimum tension known as Tone in the muscles. This minimal continual contraction is very important for the maintenance of the posture.

TYPES OF CONTRACTION :

Skeletal muscles contract only when stimulated by the incoming nerve message unlike the visceral muscles which have an inherent automaticity which is only influenced by the incoming nerve message. During the action the skeletal muscle tries to contract. This contraction could be of two types; ISOTONIC and ISOMETRIC. Isotonic contraction results when the muscle fibre shortens and cause the joint to move through some range of motion against constant resistance.

On the other hand in Isometric contraction the muscle length remains the same but the muscle tension increases. It tightens up the muscle but does not produce movement.

Normally most of the body actions are the combination of these two. The strength of contraction in the skeletal muscle depends on the initial length of its fibres; to their metabolic condition and to the number of them contracting further. This helps in the modulation of the strength of the muscle contraction as per requirement which varies in different situation.

SOME IMPORTANT MUSCLES :

1 Spinal muscles : They are grouped round the vertebral column. They are known as Extensor muscles and are necessary for both flexion and extension movement. Not very powerful muscles are required for flexion, though abdominal muscles fill this role. But to control forward flexion of the trunk, and to pull up such a weight again back, massive extensor muscles are required which start from the back of the sacrum and adjoining parts of the pelvis and fan out into a large number of muscular strips, ascending to attachment on the vertebrae and ribs above.

IMPORTANT RESPIRATORY MUSCLES :

2 Thoracic intercostal muscles

These are the small muscles in between the ribs. The external intercostal muscles elevate the ribs in inspiration while internal intercostal lower them during expiration.

3 Thoracic diaphragm

It is a dome shaped muscular sheet which separates the thoracic cavity from the abdominal cavity. When it contracts, it becomes flat pulling down at its central tendon, thus increasing the vertical diameter of the thorax, and when it is relaxed it rises again regaining its original dome shape.

4 Abdominal muscles

The front wall of the abdominal cavity is formed by the sheet of number of muscles. Two important muscles are the Rectus muscles on either side of the midline which run vertically from the lower border of the chest upto pubic symphysis. Other muscles form the side wall of the abdominal cavity.

5 Pelvic floor

At the base of the abdominal cavity are group of muscles which form a muscular floor, pierced by the anal opening, along with the urethral opening in male and vaginal opening in female. It has an important role in the Pranayamic breathing.

PSYCHOSOMATIC CONCEPTS :

Here it would be worthwhile to know the intimate relationship between the mind and the muscles. The mind continuously tries to express itself through the facial expressions, gestures and the postures. It uses continuously the Skeletal muscles to express itself. Thus mind continuously uses the muscles and one should bear in mind that if it can use it, it can misuse it too. The continuous excitement, agitation, depression in the mind keeps the muscles continuously tense and over worked. And as with the skeletal muscles it is equally true with the visceral muscles as well. Thereafter from the continuous tension in the visceral muscles it is only next step to various functional disorders of those visceral organs. The level of functioning of the internal organs as a whole is known as postural substrate. This is continuously influenced by the state of mind. Any long term disturbance in the mind influences the postural substrate adversely leading to various disorders which are termed as PSYCHOSOMATIC DISEASES e.g. high blood pressure, peptic ulcer, gastritis etc. Over the period, this disturbed pattern of postural substrate gets fixed and even in the absence of any mental disturbance; contributes continuously to the internal disfunction. Unless this pattern is changed and new pattern is established, just a simple psycho-therapeutic procedure would not help in the treatment of these disorders. Yogic physical culture, tries to modify the old faulty pattern and also tries to establish a new pattern as far as this postural substrate is concerned. When simultaneously a Yogic Mental Culture is also adopted then it becomes one of the most effective tools for the treatment of psychosomatic disorders.

NERVOUS SYSTEM

GENERAL CONSIDERATION

To control and coordinate the functions of the far flung areas of the body it is essential that there should be a system for rapid communication between these areas and which can also act as a controlling agency to coordinate and integrate the various functions of the body. NERVOUS SYSTEM along with the ENDOCRINE SYSTEM is chiefly responsible for this control and integration of the body functions.

On the basis of structure this nervous system can be distinguished into a central part constituting the brain and the spinal cord known as CENTRAL NERVOUS SYSTEM and the peripheral nerves with the sensory organs forming the PERIPHERAL NERVOUS SYSTEM.

Functionally on the other hand nervous system can be divided into two parts; the one which concerns with the control of voluntary actions is known as SOMATIC NERVOUS SYSTEM and for the control of autonomous visceral function, known as AUTONOMIC NERVOUS SYSTEM. Both these systems are inter-linked and share some of the structures jointly.

I : SOMATIC NERVOUS SYSTEM

The Brain : the most important part of the Central and Somatic Nervous System is the chief organiser of the whole body. It has three parts : CEREBRUM OR LARGE BRAIN, CEREBELLUM or SMALL BRAIN and BRAIN STEM, the lower most part which continues downwards is a spinal cord. The brain is made up of millions of nerve cells which make multiple contacts with each other forming unparalleled gigantic network of the nerve cells and its processes. This gives the unique richness to the mental functioning of the human beings.

The brain can compare the current situation with others in past. Incoming information can be pooled, and also compared with previous impressions, before a response is formulated and signalled to muscles. Man is able to build a conception of the world and himself, through the activities of the brain alone. This highly evolved organ has given him the capacity for perceiving the relationships between things, of inventing symbols for them, is responsible for the accumulation of an enormous treasury of thoughts, ideas and concepts which has led to innumerable handicraft, arts and sciences.

Intelligence is not perhaps peculiar to humans, but is immensely more developed in him. Dominance depends partly on strength, but intelligent skill has been proved to be more successful. Increasing skill demands greater sensory precision, finer control of muscles and hence more numerous peripheral nerve fibres. But the CENTRAL NERVOUS SYSTEM itself is the site of the greatest changes, especially the brain, where connector nerve cells accumulate in ever more elaborate connections between senses and muscles.

During the growth period, the brain cells can multiply and increase the contacts with each other only in the early childhood. By the age of 8 years the brain growth is more or less complete. If during this period i.e. either in the mother's womb or in the infancy if the child does not get good nutrition the growth of the brain will be affected. This will lead to the disturbance in the brain function of varying degrees.

SOME OF THE IMPORTANT FEATURES OF THE BRAIN FUNCTIONS

1 Ceaseless Activity :

From the time the brain develops in its primitive form in the foetus, it works ceaselessly till the death. Even in the sleep it works continuously. Its electrical activity recorded in the graphical form is known as EEG. This graph is in the wave form and depending on the frequency and the amplitude of the wave form and depending on the frequency and the amplitude of the wave different patterns of waves are recognised. When the brain is very busy in thinking or in calculation and when the eyes are open, the waves are of short amplitude and have a frequency of 13 to 25 cycles per second (c.p.s.). These are

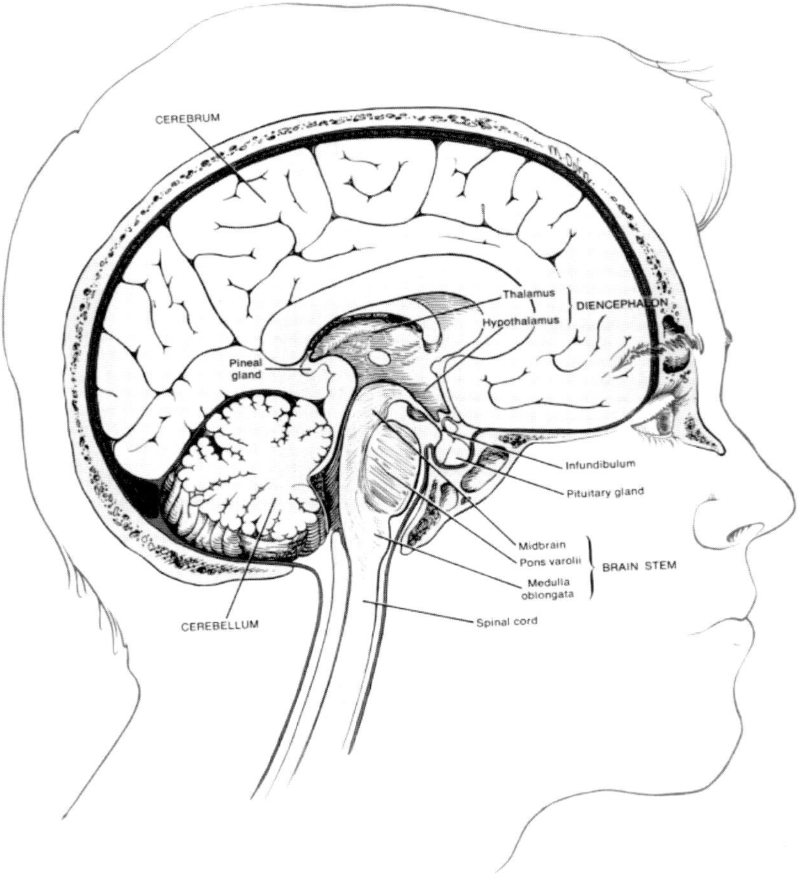

Fig. 7 Brain - Prinicpal parts of the medial aspect of the brain seen in Sagittal Section

known as Beta waves. (2) When the person is alert but restful and with the eyes closed, the waves are slightly larger and have a frequency of 8 to 12 c.p.s. These are known as Alpha waves. (3) When the person feels drowsy, the waves become still larger and the frequency is reduced to 3 to 7 c.p.s. These are known as Theta waves. (4) During deep sleep these waves become more slow and large with the frequency of less than 3 c.p.s. They are known as Delta waves. Thus by studying these wave pattern in the EEG, one can get the idea as to the level of consciousness with which the brain is functioning. During the meditative state the person usually feels relaxed, alert, minimally disturbed and this is reflected in the EEG in the form of increased Alpha waves.

2. INTEGRATIVE FUNCTIONS :

The brain perceives the sensation brought in by the sensory nerves from the peripheral sensory organs. It also initiates the motor action for which the messages are sent to the peripheral motor organs through the motor nerves. But apart from that the most important thing which the brain does, is to interpret the sensation and integrate it with the information retrieved from the memory before initiating the action. There are four major aspects of this integrative functions of the brain.

A) Consciousness : It can be defined as a state of awareness of one's own self in relation to one's environment and of other beings. The level of consciousness varies from time to time. This variation has a basic cyclicity which is known as basic rest activity cycle (BRAC). Under the influence of this cycle one passes the time either in the wakeful state or in the sleep state. Again in the wakeful state sometimes one is highly alert and attentive or relaxed and not attentive. In the sleep state too, two different states could be distinguished. One is the state of deep sleep and other is the state associated with dreaming.

Apart from the above normal BRAC there could be altered state of consciousness which occurs either under the influence of certain drugs, or during the disease or during brain injury leading to coma, or during meditative state in YOGA.

B) MEMORY : It is one of the major integrative functions of the brain associated with the left-over impression of the past experiences. Though the exact mechanism of how the brain remembers is not known it is clear from various experiments that it does not reside in any one part of the brain but is rather diffusely spread out in different parts of the brain.

C) SPEECH FUNCTION : It consists of the use of language (speaking and writing). Though certain areas of the brain seem to be more intimately associated with these functions known as speech centre, it requires the participation of many more areas of the brain. Injury to any of these areas would lead to a defect in either understanding of the speech or in the use of speech.

D) EMOTION : Specific area of the brain known as the limbic system is basically involved in the feelings as well as in the expression of the emotion. This limbic system also be comes a contact point for the somatic and visceral nervous system on one hand and the nervous and endocrine system on other. So virtually it becomes a nodal point for the functioning of the whole of neuro-endocrine system.

3. SPECIFIC FUNCTIONING OF THE DIFFERENT AREAS :

In the central nervous system one observes the division of labour. Areas in the spinal cord and the brain stem carry out their functions which are REFLEXIVE in nature. On the other hand the higher cortical functions are concerned with VOLITIONAL activities about which one is usually aware. Reflexive actions are responsible mainly for the maintenance of homoeostasis and carry out their functions without entering the field of awareness.

In both the hemisphere of the large brain or cerebrum, certain of the symmetrical areas are found to be concerned with some specific functions. The area in front of the central sulcus, functions mainly as general somatic motor area which sends out the impulses to stimulate the somatic muscles. While the area just posterior to this sulcus functions as general somatic sensory area and receives the impulses from the peripheral receptors located all over the body concerning the feeling of the heat, cold, or touch. The area in the Temporal lobe of the brain is more concerned with the hearing. While the area in the Occipital lobe is more concerned with the visions. But it is important to remember that no part of the brain functions alone in isolation, but works in coordination and in integrative manner with the other areas.

These two hemispheres also show some interesting differences in their functions. Though basically the left hemisphere controls the activity of the right side of the body and vice versa, the difference in their function concerns with some of integrative functions. The left hemisphere appears to be more concerned with the production, perception and understanding of spoken words, and also with gestures associated with the use of speech. On the other hand the right hemisphere seems to have some dominant role in the perception of non-speech sounds such as melodies, coughing, crying, laughing and in the perception of tactile sensations.

FUNCTION OF THE CEREBELLUM OR SMALL BRAIN :

The Cerebellum or the Small brain has the important role in the maintenance of body posture. It helps in the skilled movements by coordinating the activities of group of muscles. It functions below the level of consciousness to make the movements smooth instead of jerky, steady instead of trembling, and efficient and coordinated instead of ineffective, awkward and uncoordinated.

PERIPHERAL NERVES AND SENSATION :

There are 12 pairs of nerves which arise in the brain and come out through the CRANIAL cavity and there 31 pairs of nerves which come out through the Intervertebral Foramina of the spinal column. Majority of them are the combination of motor and sensory nerves.

The sensory nerves bring in the sensation from various sensory organs situated in all the parts of the body. The sensations can be broadly classified as EXTEROCEPTIVE sensation concerned with the environment and the various objects situated outside the body, and ENTEROCEPTIVE sensations concerned with the changes taking place inside the body. The enteroceptive sensation are of two types; PROPRIOCEPTIVE - concerning the movements in the various joints and the related body positions, and VISCEROCEPTIVE - concerning the sensation coming from the various visceral organs. In the normal circumstances only a small part of the exteroceptive sensations enter the field of our awareness. Rest of the exteroceptive sensation as well as more or less the whole of the enteroceptive sensation usually are not allowed to enter in the domain of consciousness but are rather used by the lower centres of the nervous system. They play a very important role by providing the information on the basis of which the body can determine when and what action is to be taken without disturbing the field of consciousness. In Yoga the awareness of these internal sensations is considered as a key to the higher awareness of the self. It is increased by the various Yogic practices viz. Asanas, Pranayama, and Mudras and through this, the effort is made to gain conscious control over the various internal activities.

II THE AUTONOMIC NERVOUS SYSTEM

TWO DIVISIONS OF AUTONOMIC NERVOUS SYSTEMS :

The regulation of the activities of the internal organs which are usually carried out autonomously is the concern of the Autonomous Nervous System. It has two divisions : SYMPATHETIC and PARA SYMPATHETIC, responsible for the opposing effect on the organs controlled by them. Most of the visceral organs are supplied by the nerves from both these divisions. And by counter-balancing the effect of each other, they regulate the functioning of the visceral organs and help in restoration of the homoeostasis.

The sympathetic system plays a dominant role in the situation of the STRESS. As a reaction to the stress where all the functions of the body are geared up to cope with the strain, the sympathetic division

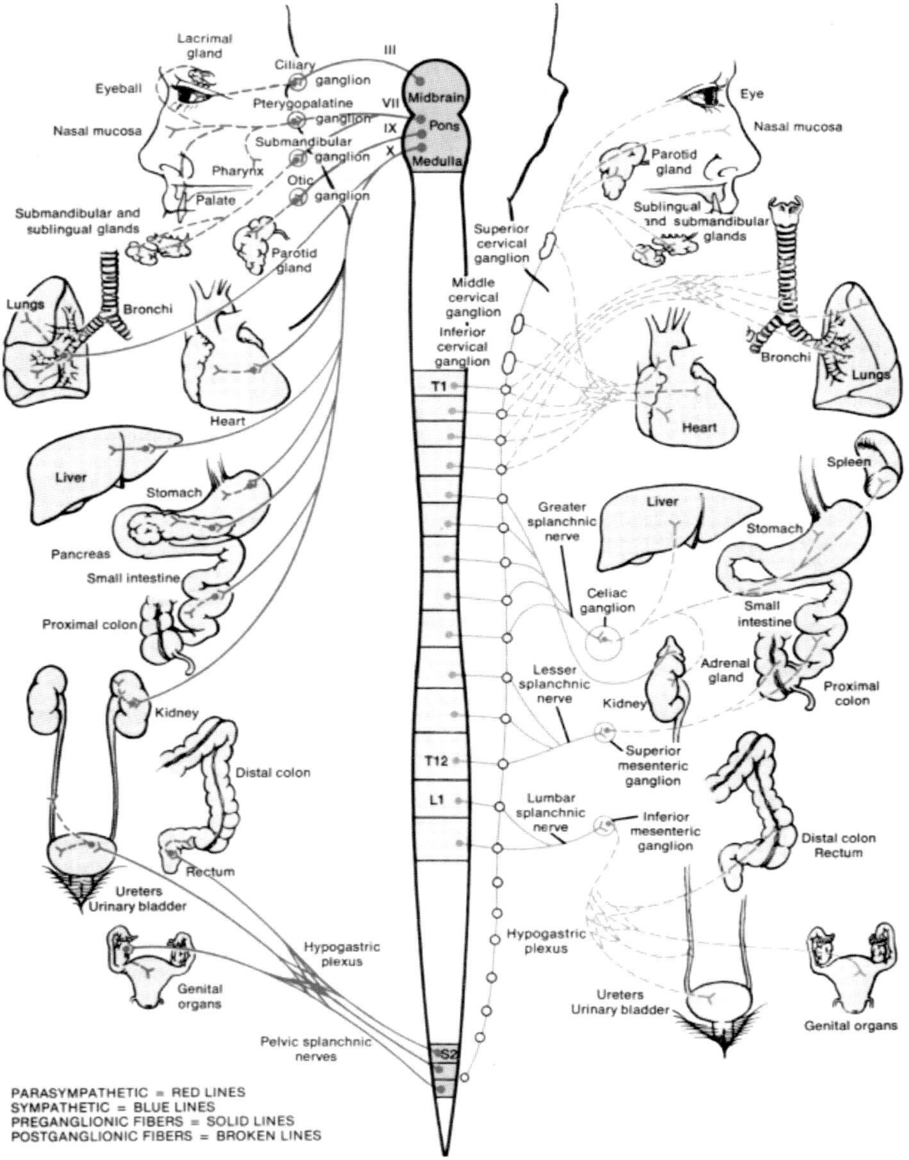

Fig. 8 Structure of the Autonomic Nervous System

predominates which increases the heart rate, blood pressure oxygen consumption, respiration and gives rise to a feeling of tenseness. On the other hand the para-sympathetic systems predominates in resting peaceful condition. This becomes very obvious in a relaxed state brought out by the Yogic practices.

BIOFEED BACK TECHNIQUE :

Though most of the visceral function are autonomous and are independent of the control from the higher brain centres, they can be influenced by will power, though may not be directly. It is possible to learn to make the visceral organ react in a specific way by following certain techniques. In the Bio-Feedback technique one becomes aware of the visceral sensations by using some audiovisual signals and then to direct signals, and by making them appear or disappear, one learns to influence the function of that organ. By using such instruments one can control the blood pressure, the body temperature or even the wave pattern of the brain.

In Yoga without taking a recourse to changing of these internal sensations into perceivable audio-visual signals; one does it by increasing the field of awareness. Thus by increasing the area of awareness and bringing into it, the whole field of internal activities; the door is opened for the subjective wilful control of the whole of the internal environment. Using the various techniques of Yogic practices one can learn more and more about the functioning of the internal organs and in its wake, can learn to control and regulate it.

ENDOCRINE SYSTEM

HORMONES

The Endocrine system consists of different glands which releases secretions directly into the blood stream. These secretions known as HORMONES circulate all over the body and help in the control of various activities. Just like the nervous system, it communicates, controls and integrates the functions all over the body, but with some difference. The nerve impulse produces rapid short lasting responses

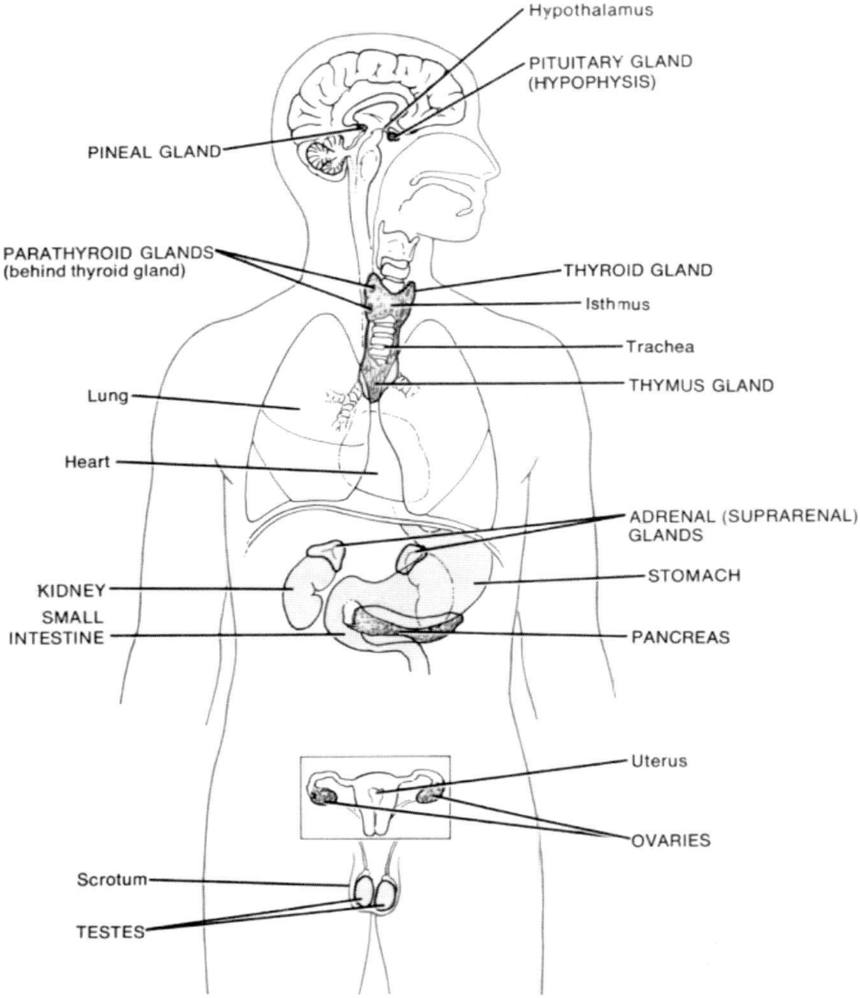

Fig. 9 Location of many Endocrine Glands and Associated Structures

but the hormones produce slower and generally long lasting response. The nerve impulse can influence only the muscle cells and gland cells while hormones influences all kinds of cells. Nerves can get fatigued more easily and are unsuitable for protracted stimulation. Where organs are to be governed for long period, it is much effective and easier to govern them through chemical means i.e. HORMONES.

INTEGRATION AT NEURO-ENDOCRINE LEVEL :

The pituitary gland produces various hormones which influence and regulate the activity of the other endocrine glands viz. Thyroid, Para-Thyroid, Adrenal, Pancreas, Ovaries in females and Testis in males. In return this pituitary gland is intimately connected through the hypothalamus with the limbic system or the emotional brain. This inter-linking of the endocrine and the nervous system ultimately integrates all the functions of the human body in one composite force. Whether it is conscious or unconscious, volitional or the vegetative, rapidly changing or enduring, all these activities in the human body are integrated in one whole, through these neuro-endocrine systems.

RESPIRATORY SYSTEM

RESPIRATION :

All the living cells require energy for carrying out its life-activities. This energy is obtained by chemical break-down of the food in the presence of oxygen. This is known as tissue respiration or the internal respiration.

food + oxygen -- carbon dioxide + water + energy.

The process through which the oxygen from the atmosphere is brought into blood stream and simultaneously the carbon dioxide and the water vapour produced in the process of tissue respiration is released into atmospheric air is known as external respiration. For this purpose the respiratory system is constructed with a large

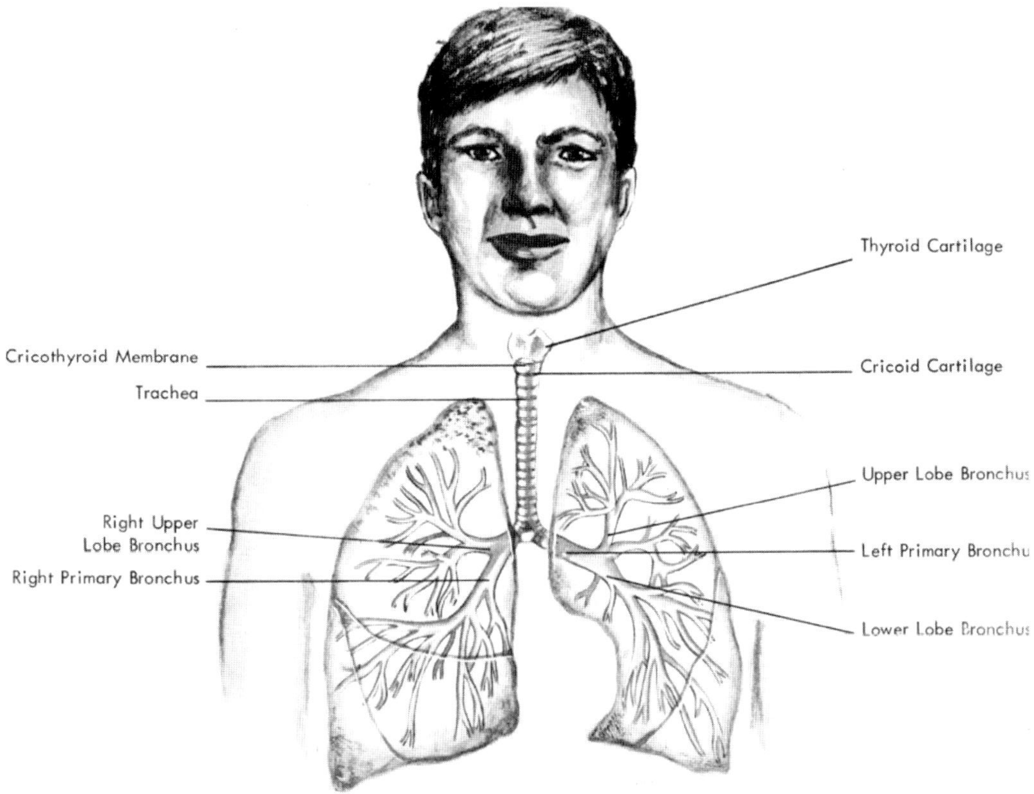

Fig. 10 The Lower Respiratory Tract

respiratory surface, approximately 80 times that of the exterior of the body, across which the exchange of oxygen, carbon dioxide etc. can take place. Simultaneously for transferring these gases from the respiratory surface to the tissues, respiratory system has to depend on the very close cooperation with the circulatory system.

The organs of the respiratory system are Nose, Pharynx, Larynx, Trachea, Bronchi, Bronchiole, the Alveolar ducts and Alveoli. The salient features of the structure of each are as follows :

NOSE :

The external nose is the visible part of the nose, but its most important part is the inner nasal cavity. The nasal cavity is divided into two halves by the vertical nasal septum. In each half of the nasal cavity are horizontal projections known as Turbinates. Cavities in the bone surrounding the nasal cavity itself are known as Para Nasal Sinuses and each of the latter communicates through some opening with the nasal cavity. Also the Naso-Lacrimal duct opens into the nasal cavity through which tears (lacrimal secretions) produced in the eyes, flow down in the nose. Whole of the Nasal cavity along with the para-nasal sinuses and the naso-lacrimal duct are lined internally by the nasal mucosa. This nasal mucosa contains numerous glands which on stimulation produce sticky secretions. The cells of the nasal mucosa also have the finger like microscopic ciliary projections which by their continuous movements make the secretions produced by the mucosal glands, flow down towards the throat. Underneath the mucosa are numerous blood capillaries which are supplied by the autonomic nerve fibres. When these blood vessels dilate, more amount of blood is brought in, that area which leads to the swelling of the mucosal lining and there by reducing the internal space causing the congestion in nasal cavity.

The main function of the nasal cavity is to condition the air by bringing it to body temperature and humidifying it. It also acts as a seat of organ for the smell. The olfactory nerves come in contact with the smell-particles floating in the incoming air which leads to smell perception.

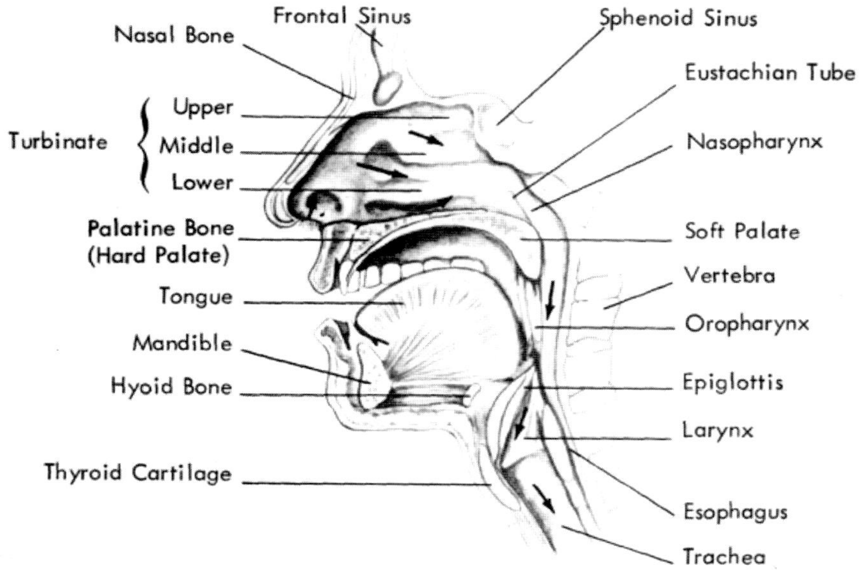

Fig. 11 The Upper Respiratory Tract

PHARYNX :

The throat or the pharynx is an important functional area. The nasal cavity through its two posterior openings joins the upper part of the throat. Also the Eustachian tube from the middle ear of the each side, opens into the throat. Also the oral cavity opens into the throat. In its lower part oesophagus and the larynx have their openings. Thus it becomes one of the important junctions along which the food and air has to pass. It also helps in the phonation.

LARYNX :

The Larynx or the voice box lies at the upper end of the trachea just below the pharynx. The mucus membrane which lines the larynx forms a pair of folds that juts inwards into its cavity. These folds are known as vocal cords, and the slit like opening between these cords is known as GLOTTIS. By closing or opening of the glottis the passage of the air can be controlled. The vibrations produced in the vocal cords by out-going air when glottis is partially closed produces the voice. By closing glottis completely the exit of the air can be controlled and the intra-thoracic pressure can be increased and maintained at the high level, as in coughing or during Kumbhaka Process of Pranayama. On the other hand the closing of the glottis also prevents the entry of the air from outside even when the intra-thoracic pressure is lowered as in Uddiyana kriya.

TRACHEA, BRONCHUS AND LUNGS :

The air passage continues down into a Trachea-the wind pipe which divides itself into two : left and right bronchus, which in turn divides further and still further eventually terminating in microscopic branches which open up in the alveolar sacs, the walls of which consist of numerous alveoli. Around three hundred million alveoli are estimated to be present in our lungs.

GAS EXCHANGE :

Alveolar wall forms the real respiratory surface across which the actual gas exchange takes place. On one side of the alveolar wall is the air and on the other side is the blood flowing through the capillary. The blood which flows along the wall of the alveolus absorbs oxygen from it and gives out the carbon dioxide to the air inside alveoli. The air is constantly circulated through the alveolar sac, brought in through the air passages known as bronchiolar tree.

In the wall of the bronchiolar tree are the small cartilaginous pieces which due to their firmness help it remain open. There are also small muscles attached to this cartilages. When these muscles contract, the air passage become constricted as sometimes happen in the case of Bronchial Asthma and is called Bronchospasm. Additionally the internal lining of this air passage which resembles that of the nose can get swollen and can produce a thick mucoid secretions. This can further reduce the internal diameter of the air passage. Therefore for the passage of the air to remain clear it is very much essential that the muscles in the air passage do not contract, the mucosal lining does not get swollen up and does not produce more than normal secretion.

Otherwise the breathing becomes difficult affecting the gaseous exchange in the alveoli.

MECHANICS OF BREATHING :

During the process of breathing the internal volume of the chest cage is alternately increased and decreased by the movement of the diaphragm and the ribs. In the quiet breathing the actual events which take place are as follows

BREATHING IN = INSPIRATION

1 The diaphragm contracts and flattens down increasing the vertical diameter of the thoracic cage.

2 The intercostal muscles contract and move the ribs up and out increasing the horizontal diameter of the thoracic cage.

3 Volume of thorax (and therefore of the lungs) increases, and its internal pressure falls below atmospheric pressure.

4 Atmospheric pressure forces air into lungs.

BREATHING OUT = EXHALATION

1 The diaphragm relaxes and moves up.

2 The intercostal muscles relax and ribs move down decreasing the horizontal diameter of thoracic cage.

3 Volume of thorax (and therefore of the lungs) thus decreases and its internal pressure increases above atmospheric pressure.

4 As a result of this, air is forced out of the lungs.

During more elaborate breathing, especially during expiration, some muscles can actively aid expiration by contracting. Abdominal wall and the muscles of pelvic floor, for example can contract and by increasing the intra-abdominal pressure can push the relaxing diaphragm upward much more than in quiet breathing.

In average condition, breathing is fairly gentle activity, but when occasion demands the respiratory muscles are capable of much greater force.

LUNG VOLUMES :

The lungs cannot be empty completely even at the end of maximum and forceful expiration and what remains behind is known as Residual volume (approximately 1 litre). In quiet breathing the amount of air taken in and out of the lungs in known as TIDAL VOLUME (approximately 500cc) while the maximum amount of air which can be taken in and out of the lungs is known as vital capacity. (approximately 3-4 litres). The amount of the air breathed in one minute is known as minute ventilation. It depends on the respiration rate and the tidal volume.

CONTROL OF RESPIRATION :

The normal spontaneous respiration takes place without the intervention of consciousness and is governed by complex nervous control system with both chemical as well as neural messages brought to it. It regulates the rhythmic breathing pattern and adjusts the minute ventilation to match the needs of gas exchange which vary according to the change in the internal metabolic demand. But the respiration may also get altered automatically during the act of speaking and singing, or it may get affected by emotions as in the act of laughing and crying, or it may get modified by reflexes as in sneezing and coughing. One can also voluntarily alter the respiration as in breath holding or in Pranayamic breathing.

The respiration has also an important role to play in the control of the body temperature, in immune response by producing some specific antibodies, and in filtering hormones and blood cells. In Pranayamic breathing lung volumes are manipulated consciously over a wide range along with the manipulation of intra-thoracic and intra-abdominal pressures, thereby affecting enormously all these functions.

CIRCADIAN RHYTHM OF RESPIRATION :

It is important to know that respiratory system is also influenced by the rhythmic variation during each 24 hour period of day-and-night cycle. This rhythmic change in breathing pattern is also linked to Basic Rest Activity Cycle mentioned earlier in discussion on the function of Brain. Apart from the change in the pattern of the breathing is the cyclical change in the congestion of nasal mucosa which offers resistance to the movement of air through one particular nostril at any given time. This uni-nostrilar resistance changes rhythmically from one nostril to another every one and half to two hours.

CARDIOVASCULAR SYSTEM

CARDIOVASCULAR or the circulatory system is the only system available for the transportation of various things in the body. Blood picks up the food and water from the digestive system, Oxygen from the respiratory system and Hormone from the endocrine system; and delivers the same to different parts of the body. It also picks up waste matter from all over the body and delivers it to the excretory systems. It also distributes heat all around the body.

This circulatory system essentially consists of three parts :

(1) The blood - it is a fluid in which the various materials are carried to and from the tissues. (2) The heart - it is a driving force that propels the blood. (3) The blood vessels - these are the routes through which the blood travels to and through the tissue, and back to the heart.

A. BLOOD :

Blood consists of plasma which is a fluid part in which float different types of cells. Plasma constitutes 55 % of the total blood volume and the rest is formed by cells alone. There are three kinds of blood cells;

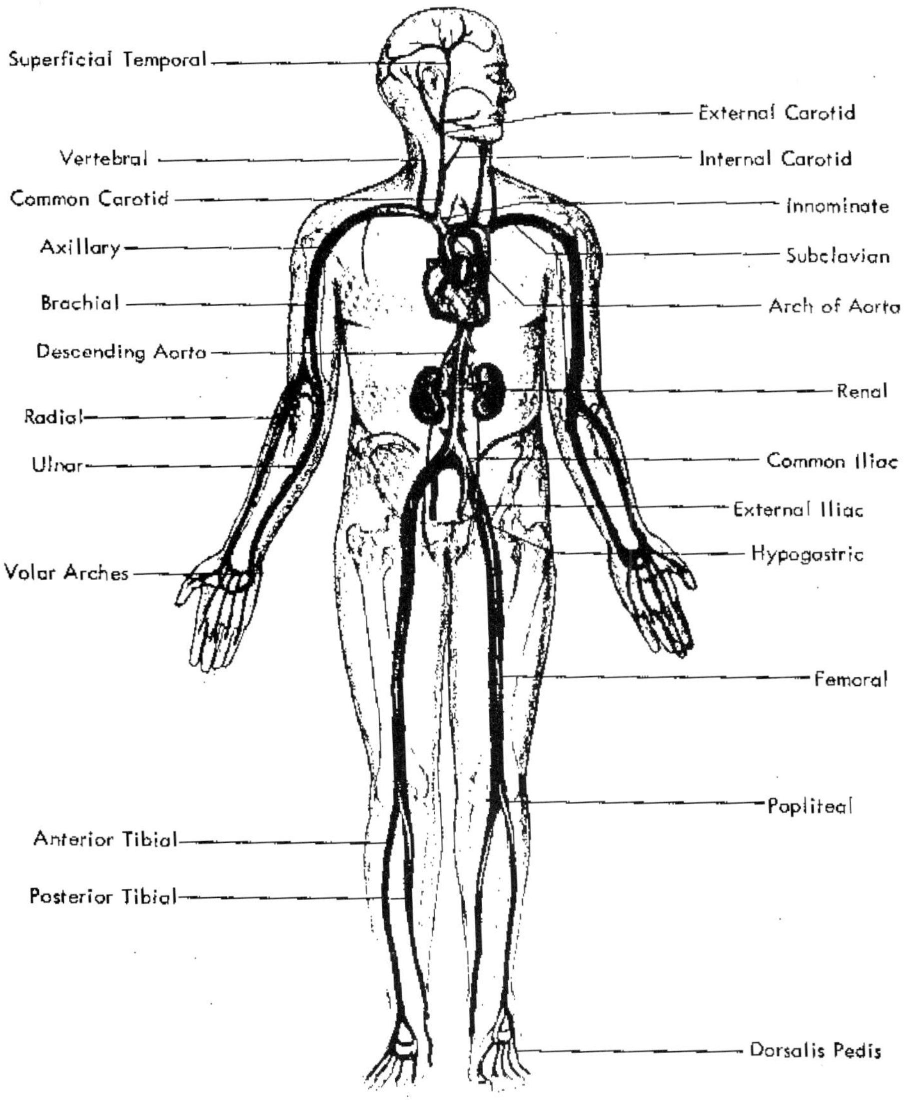

Fig. 12 Major Arteries of the Body

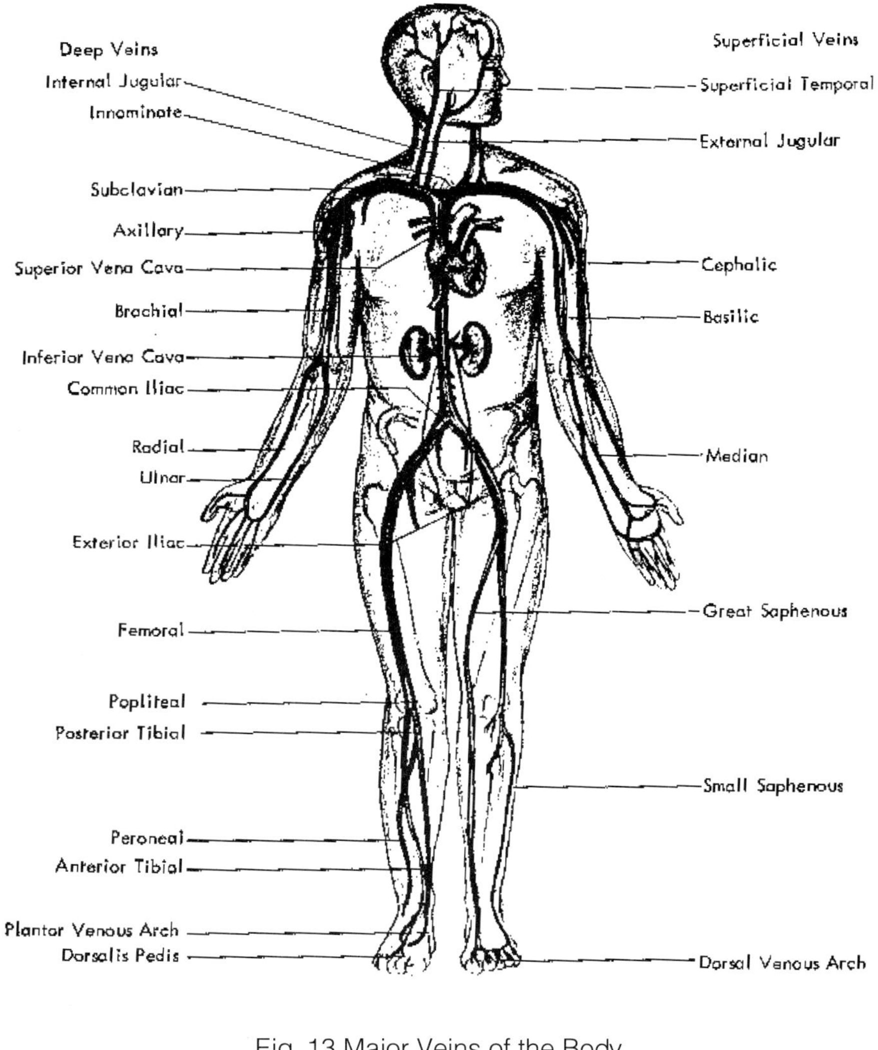

Fig. 13 Major Veins of the Body

1. RED BLOOD CELLS - These are responsible for the transport of Oxygen and Carbon-dioxide. In each cell, is packed a chemically very active agent known as Haemoglobin. In most of the normal men 100 ml. of blood contains 14 to 16 gm. of haemoglobin and in women it is 12 to 14 gm. per 100 ml. When the haemoglobin content becomes less the Oxygen carrying capacity of the blood is reduced and a person is said to be suffering the Anaemia. The red blood cells are formed in the bone marrow and have a life-span of 120 days. The hormone Erythoprotein, secreted by the kidneys, helps in maintaining the number of red cells constant at about 4.5 to 5.5. million per ml. of blood. Also the adequate amount of Vitamin B 12, Iron, Copper, Cobalt etc. helps in maintaining the red cell homoeostasis.

2. WHITE BLOOD CELLS - These cells can move in any direction and some time even out, through the wall of capillaries and can destroy the harmful micro-organisms or particles; and thus function as a part of body's defence mechanism. One of the white blood cells known as Lymphocytes play an important role in the development of immunity by producing antibodies. Most of the white cells are formed in the red bone marrow. The lymphocytic cells originate from what is known as lymphatic tissue. Normally there are 5000 to 9000 white blood cells per ml. of normal blood. When the different types of white blood cells are counted separately and their percentage is computed it is known as a differential count.

3. PLATELETS - These cells play important role in the blood clotting mechanism. These cells are formed in the red bone marrow and have a short life-span of an average of about 10 days. The blood has a unique quality. Inside the intact blood vessel it remains fluid, while on the rupture of blood vessel it coagulates to form a clot which plugs up the ruptured vessel and stops further bleeding thus preventing the loss of precious vital body fluid. The coagulation of the blood is a very complex process and requires presence of large number of factors in proper proportion.

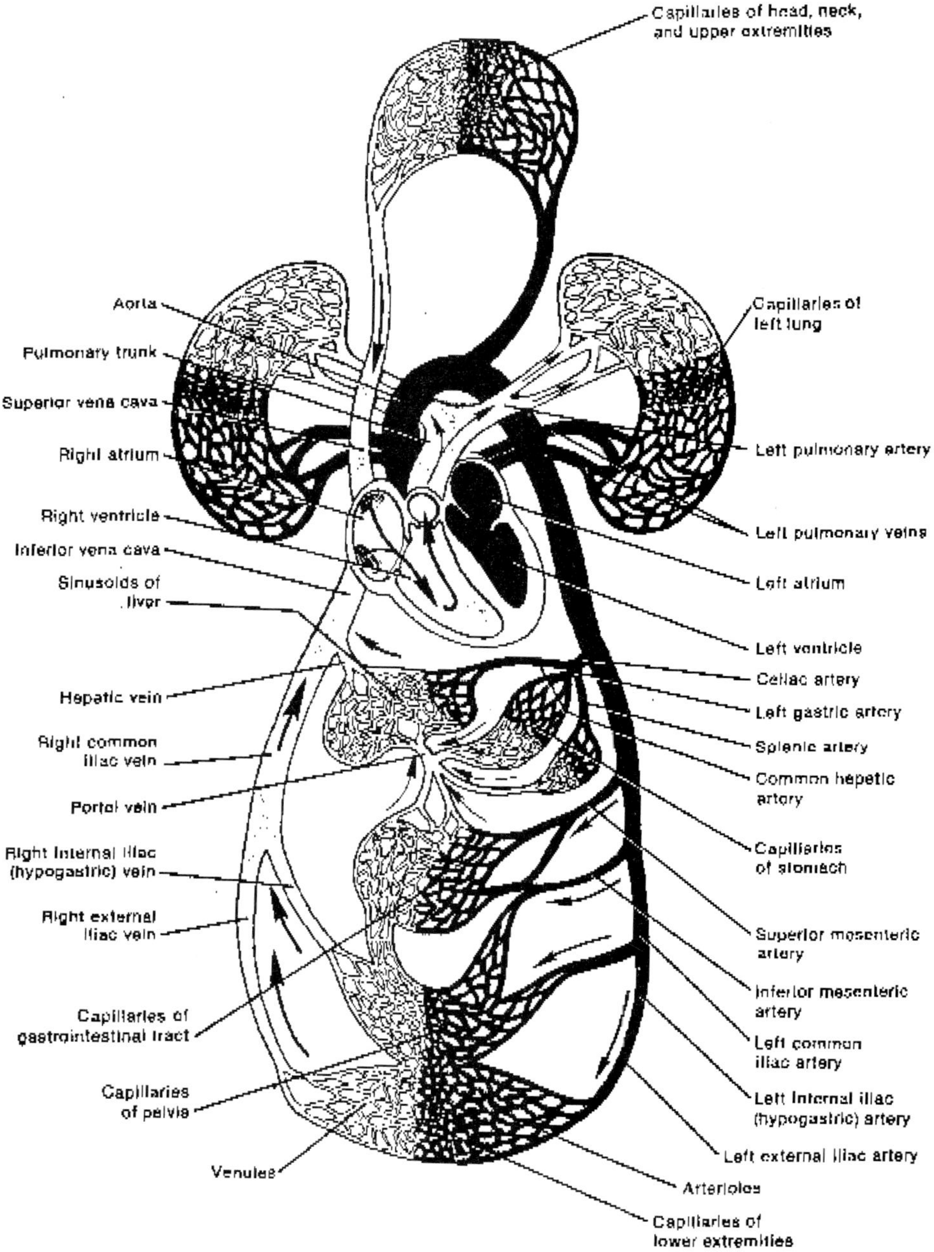

Fig. 14 The Circulatory Routes

B. HEART :

It is a muscular pump with four chambers within it. When its chambers contract it is known as SYSTOLE and when they relax it is known as DIASTOLE. This contraction and relaxation goes rhythmically and sequentially in different chambers due to the rhythmic impulse generated by the specialised neural tissue, inside the heart muscle known as SINOATRIAL node. This impulse spreads throughout the cardiac muscles and brings about the contraction of the different chambers in particular sequence. The record, of the conduction of electrical impulse inside the heart - to its various parts, in known as ELECTRO CARDIO GRAM (ECG). This inherent autonomicity of the heart is under the influence of autonomic nervous system. The increase in the sympathetic activity leads to increase in the frequency of contraction, leading to increase in the heart rate. It also increases the force of contraction leading to increase in blood pressure. Parasympathetic over activity on the other hand reduces the heart rate as well as the blood pressure.

Though the heart supplies blood to the rest of the body it requires a part of it, for its own use, too. The arteries which supply the blood to the heart are known as CORONARIES. When these coronaries narrow down because of the transient spasm or because of the permanent deposition of fatty substance inside its lumen, the blood supply to MYOCARDIAL cells is reduced and this condition is known as MYOCARDIAL ISCHEMIA. When this Ischemia becomes too severe or when the blood clot formed inside the blood vessel in some other part flows in and plugs any of the coronary artery, the blood supply to the distal part gets obstructed leading to the death of the cells and this condition is known as MYOCARDIAL INFARCTION.

C. TYPES OF BLOOD VESSELS :

There are three kinds of blood vessels : Arteries, capillaries and veins.

Blood vessels form a continuous system of tubes in which the blood is circulated, each type of vessel being continuous with the next - it is a closed system.

1 ARTERIES - They carry the oxygenated blood away from the heart (except the pulmonary artery) and have a thick layer of smooth muscles in its wall which can constrict or relax. The constriction of the arteries reduces the internal diameter and thus increases the resistance to the flow of blood. This peripheral resistance to the blood flow is an important factor, in diverting the blood flow from rest of the body parts towards the more vital organs as and when required. The blood pressure is also dependent on it. Whenever the peripheral resistance increases the blood pressure also shows the increase, and when this resistance is lowered, as by the Yogic relaxation techniques, the blood pressure comes down.

2 CAPILLARIES - Capillaries are microscopic vessels that carry blood from small arteries to small veins. Their walls are the thinnest, lined by the single layer of cells through which the oxygen and the nutrient pass out for the use of surrounding cells, and the waste matter, carbon dioxide, hormones, etc. enter in, from the surrounding cells. Thus the capillaries are the most important of blood vessels with the function of keeping cells supplied with vital material and getting rid off the injurious waste matter.

3 VEINS - These are comparatively thinner vessels which carry the deoxygenated blood (except the pulmonary veins) towards the heart. Inside the veins there are valves at intervals which open only in the direction of the heart. In the upright position when the blood is to be flown against the gravity towards the heart these valves help in dividing the column of the blood in the deeper veins into smaller units; which then further can be squeezed upwards by the contraction of the skeletal muscles around them. When these valves become defective and the venous return towards the heart is affected leading to the stagnation of the blood in the vessels itself and causing ultimately the dilation of the vessels, it leads to what is known as VARICOSITY. Apart from muscle contraction the changes in the intra abdominal pressure which occurs during the routine breathing activity also helps in VENOUS RETURN. It sucks up the Venous blood from the lower limbs into intra abdominal cavity when the pressure inside becomes negative and pushes towards the heart when the inside pressure becomes positive. Partially the suction action of the auricle when empty, also helps in making the venous blood flow back towards the heart.

CIRCULATION AND BLOOD PRESSURE - The control of the blood circulation is a very complex process. Not only the blood is to be kept in motion but it needs to be distributed in more amount with more speed and more force whenever the particular part of the body so requires. The blood pressure which keeps the blood circulating depends on two factors : the peripheral resistance and the cardiac minute output, i.e. the volume of blood pumped by the heart in one minute. This output, in its turn, depends on the heart rate as well as the force of contraction during each systole. The neural and the chemical information is continuously brought in from all over the body as well is sensed by the brain itself when the blood flows through it. This information regarding the oxygen or carbon dioxide level in the blood, volume of the blood, increase or decrease in the flow in particular area etc. helps the brain in initiating various actions which keep the blood pressure as well as the blood circulation properly regulated.

LYMPHATIC SYSTEM

When the fluid part of the blood oozes out of the blood capillaries, only 40 % of it returns back. The 60% of it which remains behind is known as the LYMPH. This is the fluid which encircles the cells and is known as INTERSTITIAL FLUID, of the body. This lymph, flows back towards the heart through lymph vessels, bringing some of the important constituents back to the blood. Any obstruction in the lymphatic drainage of any part of the body leads to OEDEMA or swelling.

Along the pathways of lymphatic vessels are the small glands known as LYMPH NODES. These are densely packed with the lymphocytes and when lymph flows through it the obnoxious particles

INTRODUCTORY ANATOMY AND PHYSIOLOGY:
THE LYMPHATIC AND RETICULOENDOTHELIAL SYSTEMS

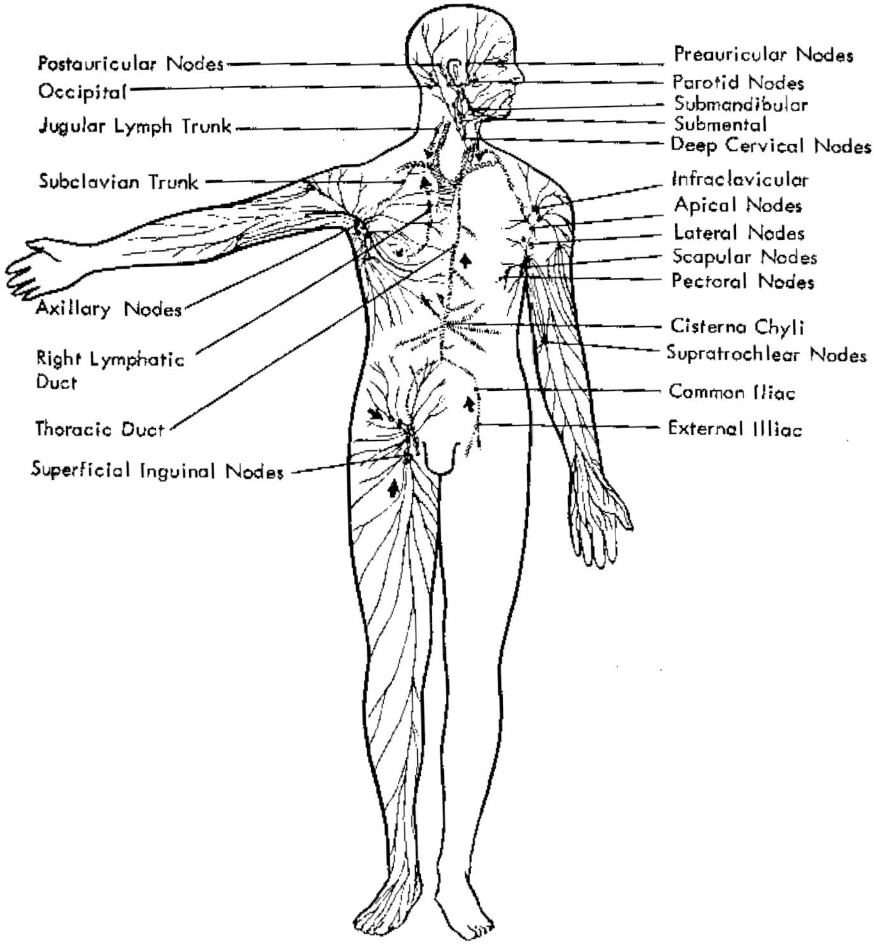

Fig. 15 The Lymphatic System

like microorganisms are filtered and destroyed by these cells. The lymphocytes also produce the antibodies and thus the lymph nodes play an important role in the defence mechanism of the body. One of the important lymph nodes situated in the throat, in known as TONSIL.

DIGESTIVE SYSTEM

Some substances in the diet can be absorbed in the blood stream without digestion e.g. mineral ions and vitamins, but the majority of the other food items eaten in their present form cannot be used by the cells as it is. Their chemical composition and physical nature needs to be modified so that it can be absorbed and utilized by the body cells. This is the function of the digestive system, additionally it also helps in the elimination of waster matter.

Structurally, the digestive system is like a tube open at both the ends. It is lined internally with the mucous membrane which contains the different glands along different parts which secretes the digestive juices of different nature. The wall of the digestive system is formed of smooth muscles arranged in circular as well as in the longitudinal fashion. Because of the contraction of these muscles the food gets churned inside the stomach, gets mixed with the gastric juice and is propelled further through the intestine. Here it is further mixed up with the other digestive juices, from the liver, pancreas and the intestine itself and after digesting the food it is absorbed into the blood, through the intestinal mucosa. Apart from the main digestive tract there are also other organs like salivary glands, liver and pancreas which produce different types of digestive juices and pour them into this tract. The production of the total digestive juices in 24 hours is about 6 lit of which 95% is re-absorbed.

THE PROCESS OF DIGESTION - Digestion is the sum of all the changes which food undergoes in the digestive tract. There are two kinds of changes, mechanical and chemical. Mechanical digestion consists in the breaking down of the large solid pieces into minute dissolved particles thereby facilitating the chemical digestion.

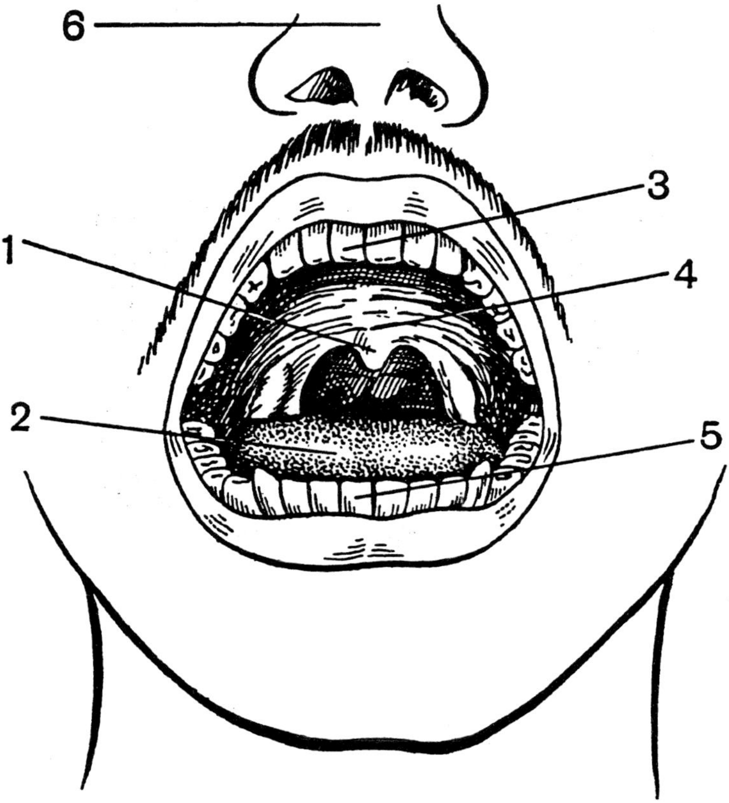

(1) The Uvula
(2) The Tongue
(3) The Upper Set of Teeth
(4) The Soft Palate
(5) The lower Set of Teeth
(6) The Nose

Fig. 16 The Mouth Widely Opened

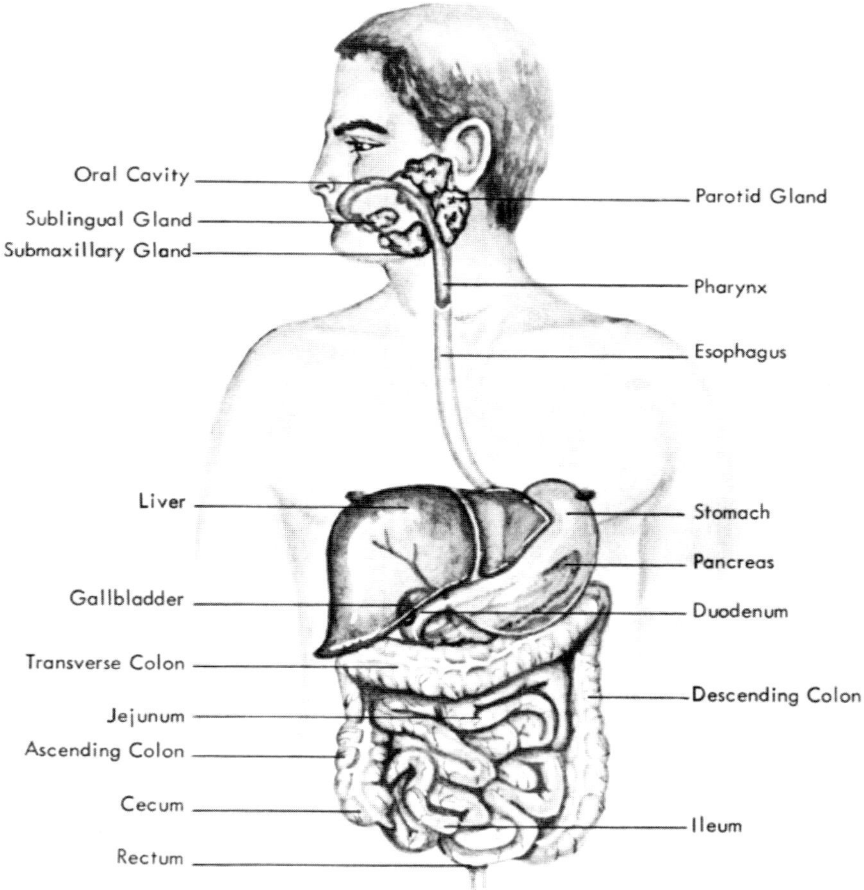

Fig. 17 The Digestive System

Chemical digestion involves the various changes which carbohydrates, proteins and the fatty content of the food undergoes, after coming in contact with saliva, gastric juice, the pancreatic juice, liver juice and the intestinal juice.

THE PROCESS OF ABSORPTION - After the food is digested it gets absorbed through the intestinal mucosa into the blood or lymph. Through the mucosal wall, not only the digested food but also the water, mineral and vitamins gain the entry into the blood circulation. This blood from the intestinal wall before getting mixed with the general circulation, travels through the liver wherein the major part of the food absorbed, gets stored for the future use. Liver also helps in changing some of the toxic substances into non-toxic form. This is known as DETOXICATION.

THE PROCESS OF METABOLISM - Foods are first digested, then absorbed and are finally metabolized. Metabolism is the actual utilization of the food by the body cells.

METABOLISM CONSISTS OF TWO MAIN PROCESSES - The process of ANABOLISM by which cells build up new material e.g. Hormones, enzymes, antibodies etc., and the CATABOLISM process through which the food is broken down to provide the energy which is required for anabolism as well as for the other kinds of cellular functions. Normally for the energy production, cells, first use the carbohydrates then the fats and lastly the proteins. The amount of energy released in the body in a given time through the process of catabolism is expressed by the term METABOLIC RATE. It actually means the rate of Energy released. The rate of energy expenditure under basal condition i.e. when the person is awake but resting, has had his previous meal atleast 12 hours before, and has a normal body temperature; i.e. does not have fever etc.; is known as BASAL METABOLIC RATE (BMR). Usually this metabolic rate in the basal condition is used as a reference; in comparison of which the metabolic rate in other condition is evaluated. In a condition when the Metabolic Rate goes up above the level of BMR it is known as hyper-metabolic state and when it is below the level of BMR it is known as hypometabolic state. The long term training in Yogic practices, has been found to influence the metabolic rate and in certain conditions, even leads to HYPOMETABOLIC state.

The total metabolic rate is the amount of energy produced or used in a given time, say in 24 hours. It includes the energy used for maintaining the life activities during basal condition as well as for the other muscular work involved in all the other routine activities of the day. It is expressed in kilo calories per hour per day.

TOTAL METABOLIC RATE AND WEIGHT CONTROL - When the energy input through the food is equal to the energy output measured by the total metabolic rate, then the Body weight remains constant. When the total calorie input exceeds energy output then the body weight increases e.g. approximately 3,500 K cal in excess can produce one pound of fatty tissue. On the other hand when the energy input is less than the energy output, the body weight decreases. Thus, anyone who wants to reduce the weight should eat fewer calories than the total metabolic rate. Unless the caloric intake is less than the caloric output, weight loss is impossible.

When the food intake is controlled drastically the stored carbohydrates in the form of glucose is used up first, completely within the first one or two days. The body starts using the accumulated fat and when this also is exhausted then the tissue proteins are catabolised rapidly with disastrous effect on the body. Therefore it is essential to know that drastic curtailment of food intake in the form of 'CRASH DIETING' as means of rapid reduction of the body weight can affect the body function adversely if, it is kept up for a prolonged period.

EXCRETORY SYSTEM

For the process of excretion of the waste matter from the body four organs are responsible, they are kidneys, intestine, skin and lungs. Kidneys excrete waste matter through urine, intestine through stool, skin through perspiration and lungs through exhaled air. Though it is essential for all the four organs to work efficiently so that the internal environment is maintained favourable for the cellular function, by far the kidneys are the most important organs amongst them.

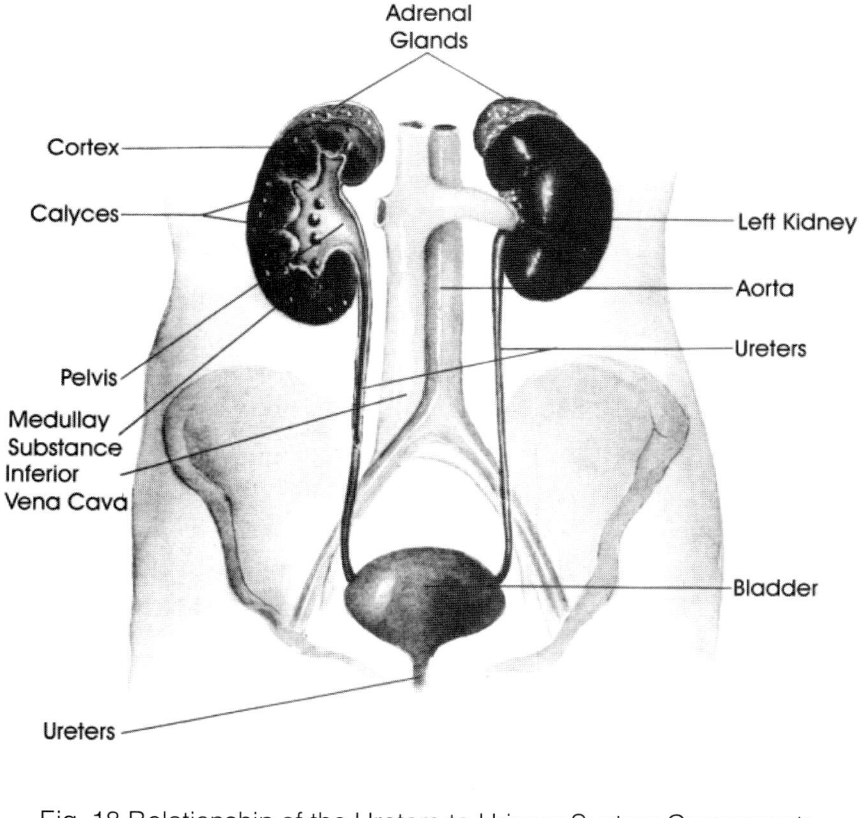

Fig. 18 Relationship of the Ureters to Urinary System Components

Kidneys can adjust the amounts of water and electrolytes leaving the body, so that they equal the amount of these substances entering the body. They help in maintaining normal concentration of various electrolytes viz. sodium, potassium, chloride etc. which are vital for the cellular activity. This has an important role in the maintenance of internal homoeostasis. The function of the kidney is influenced by two hormones : ADH produced by the Pituitary and the Aldosterone produced by the adrenal. On the other hand when the blood supply to the kidney is reduced it produces the hormone Renin-Angiotensin, which influences the blood pressure resulting in its rise, and thereby the rise in the blood supply to the kidney cells. Thus the chronic ischemia (inadequate blood supply) due to decrease in the diameter of the renal arteries can lead to permanent rise in the blood pressure known as RENAL HYPERTENSION.

REPRODUCTIVE SYSTEM

REPRODUCTION

The main reproductive tissues have a dual role. The testes in male not only produce the spermatozoa but also produce the hormone Testosterone which is responsible for the "Maleness" i.e. the male sexual characteristics and for the male sexual behaviour. Similarly ovaries in female produce not only the ovum but also produces two hormones, oestrogens and progesterone. These hormones are responsible for "Femaleness" i.e. female sexual characteristics including a cyclical change of menstruation.

THE SEXUAL BEHAVIOUR

This is an important outcome of the action of the reproductive system. The emotional content of the sexual behaviour is one of the potent factors that could influence person's physical as well as mental health. Any misgivings, distorted impressions, or faulty, notions regarding the normal sexual behaviour is sure to cause some actual disturbance in the performance of sexual activity. Majority of the sexual problems with feeling of inadequacy of sexual performance is based more on the ignorance, apprehension and faulty imagination rather than on the actual facts. Therefore, the correct scientific information regarding the normal sexual behaviour is very essential for leading a healthy life. It would help the person to maintain his personal and social life on more sound footing and would also prevent the emergence of avoidable sexual problems.

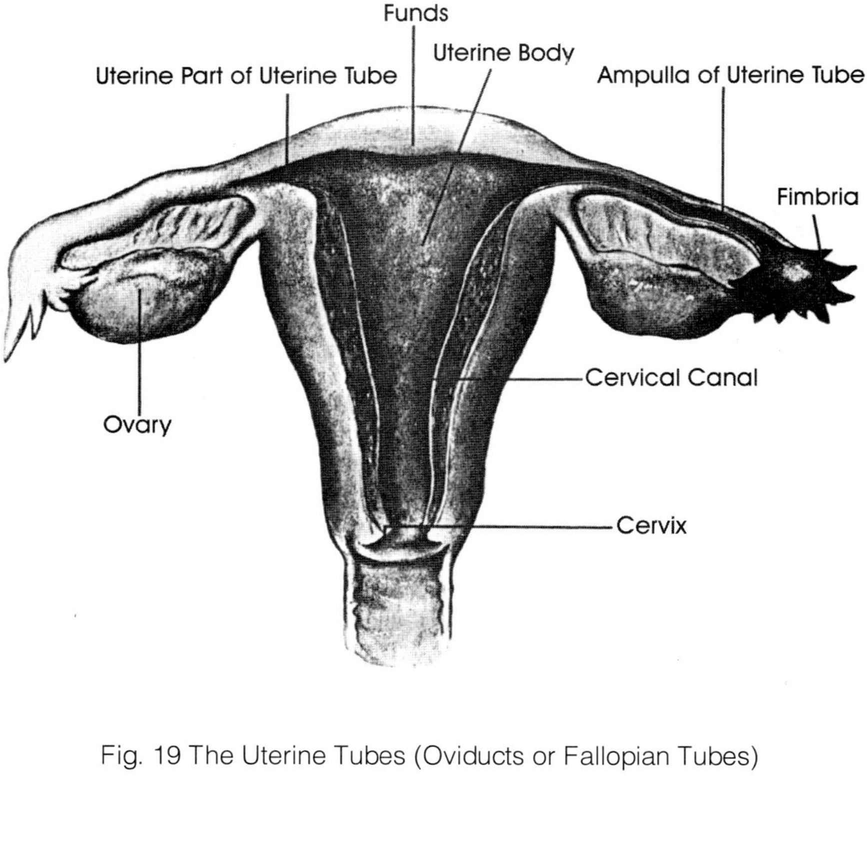

Fig. 19 The Uterine Tubes (Oviducts or Fallopian Tubes)

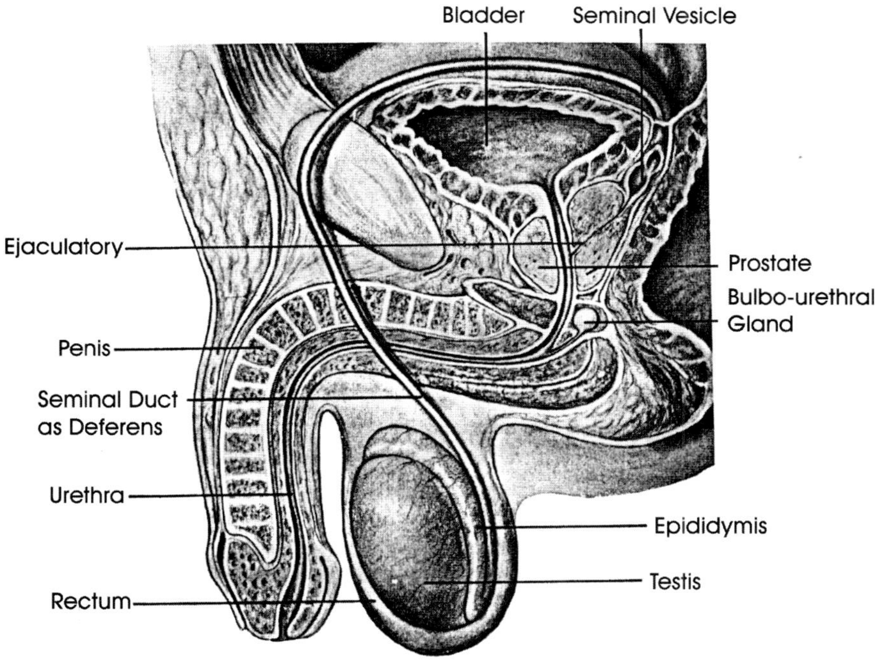

Fig. 20 Relationship of the Prostate Gland to the Urethra

PART III

REVIEW OF EFFECT OF YOGIC PRACTICES ON HUMAN BODY

REVIEW OF EFFECT OF YOGIC PRACTICES ON HUMAN BODY

The scientific research work to investigate the effects of various Yogic practices on the Human Body has been going on over last six decades. The Scientific Research Department of Kaivalyadhama, Lonavla, has a major contribution in this field. Apart from this Institute, number of research groups in India as well as in other parts of the world are engaged in this activity.

The effects of Yogic practices could be studied from two angles :

1 The immediate effect of the specific Yogic practice viz. effect of Uddiyana or Nauli kriya on the Intra-thoracic and Intra-abdominal pressure.

2 The long term effect of the group of Yogic practices performed as daily routine viz. effect of Yogic training on the physical efficiency or flexibility.

A brief summary giving only the essential aspects of the research work carried out to study the effects of various Yogic practices, either performed as a single unit or in a group; is presented below. For the sake of convenience the effects are described according to the body systems, affected by it.

EFFECT ON MUSCULOSKELETAL SYSTEM

Most of the Yogic practices, especially Asanas require fine control over the use of the muscles and the joints. The controlled use of specific group of muscles to bring about a particular movement, and the maintenance of the final position with minimum amount of muscle tone, are the two important factors in the performance of these Asanas. Because of this, all the three features of muscular activity i.e. the skill, the strength and the stamina are influenced by the Yogic practice.

Additionally the gradual and sustained increase in the range of movements through various joints increases the flexibility.

FOLLOWING ARE THE EXPERIMENTAL OBSERVATIONS

1 **ELECTRICAL ACTIVITY IN THE MUSCLES DURING THE ASANAS :**

Some of the selected Asanas were investigated for this purpose and it was observed that when the final position is maintained in a relaxed manner as recommended by Yogic texts, electrical activity in the muscles as seen in the Electro-Myogram (E.M.G.) became significantly less. On the other hand it was markedly high when the muscles were not relaxed but remained tense, with isometric contraction. For the Asanas to be effective, it is essential that the muscle-tension is kept at minimal level during the maintenance.

2 **EFFECT : MUSCLE CONDITION IN PASCHIMOTTAN, ON HEART RATE :**

When the Paschimottan was performed keeping the body musculature relaxed, the heart rate increased by 4% only. When it was done with vigorous effort to bend forward (i.e. Isotonic muscle contraction) the heart rate increased by 16%. And when it was maintained without any vigorous effort, without any relaxation in efforts but rather with tense muscles (i.e. Isometric contraction), the heart rate increased by 9%. Thus it is obvious that the Yogasanas done in a relaxed manner cause minimal strain to the heart.

3 **EFFECT OF YOGA ON STRENGTH AND ENDURANCE OF ABDOMINAL MUSCLES :**

When the person tries to sit up from the lying down position without the support of the hands it is the abdominal muscles which bring about this action. By using the sit up test in 12 females it was seen that the three weeks training in various yogasanas leads to the significant improvement in the strength and the stamina of the abdominal muscles.

4 **EFFECT OF YOGA ON FLEXIBILITY :**

By using the Cureton's flexibility test (consisting of forward flexion, backward extension should flexibility and ankle flexibility) it was found that after six weeks of training in group of Yogic practices given to 90 boys and 90 girls, the flexibility i.e. the range of movement through the various joints showed a significant increase.

5 **EFFECT OF YOGA ON STEADINESS :**

The proper coordinated use of different group of muscles leads to the steadiness in that particular part of the body. In twenty six males and eight females, the hand-steadiness showed a significant increase at the end of one month training in Yoga. The results were better in those persons who had a relaxed attitude and could do the asanas in relaxed manner.

6 **EFFECT OF YOGA ON STEADINESS AS TESTED BY MIRROR TRACING TEST :**

While the tracing the different diagrams without looking at it directly but only looking at its reflection in the mirror, one requires a steadiness of the hand as well as the steadiness of the mind. In 21 subjects who were trained in Yogic practices over the period of 8 months, the error in mirror tracing test came down significantly, from 116 to 16. In comparison to 59 errors reducing to 22 in the controlled group.

7 **EFFECT OF YOGA ON TWO HAND COORDINATION :**

By the one month training in Yoga, the mistakes in two hand coordination was found to reduce from 51 to 19 in one group of students and after 9 months of training it was found to have reduced from 48 to 29 in the other group of students. This indicated that the long term yoga training helps in the increase in the steadiness of the one particular part and also the coordination between two different parts of the body.

8 **EXTRAORDINARY MUSCLE STRENGTH BY LONG TERM YOGIC PRACTICE :**

In one subject who was practising yoga for over 30 years it was observed that he could develop the tremendous physical force to break iron chain, the links of which otherwise require a tension of 650 lbs to open up.

9 EFFECT OF YOGA ON PHYSICAL FITNESS :

By using the 'Fleishman basic fitness test' the fitness index was found to have increased significantly by 7.74 in 17 males and by 11.75 in 12 females at the end of 3 weeks training in yoga.

10 EFFECT OF YOGIC TRAINING ON MINIMUM MUSCULAR FITNESS :

To judge the muscular fitness 'Kraus Webers test' was used. When subjected to this test it was found that 40% of the school boys between age of 6 to 20 years failed in one or more items of this minimal muscular fitness test, indicating poor fitness. After the 3 weeks of yogic training when the test was repeated it showed an improvement of 36.8%.

Thus from the above observations it becomes quiet clear that when done in proper manner, yogic practices improve muscular skill (steadiness and coordination), strength and stamina as well as the flexibility. It also improves general physical fitness.

INTERNAL PRESSURE CHANGES

Number of important organs are situated inside the thoracic cavity and abdominal cavity. During certain yogic practices various parts of the chest and abdomen are manipulated which lead to the rise or fall in the pressure over these organs. These variations in the internal pressure can be judged by the rubber balloon inside the oesophagus, stomach, colon or urinary bladder, and attaching this balloon to manometer filled with water or mercury, it can also be deduced by studying the x ray plates taken during varying stages of these practices.

FOLLOWING ARE THE EXPERIMENTAL OBSERVATIONS:

1 **INCREASE IN THE INTRA-GASTRIC PRESSURE BY VARIOUS ASANAS:**

By using the intra-gastric balloon inside the stomach, the pressure was found to rise from 10 to 100 mm Hg during various asanas. The rise was marked in DHANURASAN, NAUKASAN, MAYURASAN, YOGA MUDRA and SHIRASHASANA. The rise was moderate in BHUJANGASANA, SHALABHASANA and ARDHA-MATSYENDRASANA and it was minimal in CHAKRASA and VAKRASANA. It is essential to keep this effects in mind while teaching these practices to persons suffering from Hypertension, enlarged heart, enlarged liver, or hiatus hernia as all these practices which increase the internal pressure tremendously would be harmful to them and therefore, are contra-indicated. Even those practices in which the rise is moderate, need to be done with full precaution.

2 **INCREASE IN THE INTRA-GASTRIC PRESSURE DURING GAJKARNI :**

After deep inhalation during which the diaphragm descends maximally, if the upper abdominal wall is suddenly contracted, it leads to sudden rise in the intra-gastric pressure (+ 90 to 120 mm Hg). This sudden rise in the pressure helps in opening the cardiac sphincter and to force out the content of the stomach. This is known as Gajkarni Kriya.

3 **DECREASE IN INTRA-GASTRIC PRESSURE :**

Because of the Mock-inhalation in Uddiyana in which at the end of complete exhalation thoracic cage expands and the diaphragm rises up further the intra-gastric pressure becomes negative (-25 to -29 mm Hg). This decrease in the pressure becomes more accentuated in Central Nauli (-40 to 43 mm Hg) and right and left Nauli (-37 to -40 mm Hg). Similarly the intra-colonic pressure was also found to decrease (-33 to -47 mm hg) during central Nauli. This particular partial vacuum was discovered for the first time by Swami Kuvalayananda in 1924 and was named by him as

MADHAVDAS Vacuum in memory of his Guru. He postulated that this negative pressure is responsible for suction of water in the colon during Basti Kriya and not the anti-peristalsis as hypothesised by others.

4 WATER SUCTION DUE TO NEGATIVE PRESSURE IN DIFFERENT CAVITIES:

Because of the negative pressure developed during Uddiyana in different cavities it was found that 360 ml of water gets sucked through the tube into the stomach and 45 ml in urinary bladder. But the negative pressure inside the colon was minimal and no water was sucked in. On the other hand during central Nauli the development of the negative pressure was much more than in Uddiyana leading to sucking in of 500 ml of water into the stomach, 90 ml of water in urinary bladder and 250 ml of water in colon.

5 MANIPULATION OF STOMACH AND INTESTINE DUE TO NAULI :

During the X ray studies using the barium meal it was observed that the practice of Nauli-chalan moves the position of stomach as well as the small and large intestine inside the abdominal cavity and also causes the re-distribution of its contents, thus affecting the digestive function.

6 PRESSURE CHANGES IN AGNISARA :

After deep exhalation when the breath is retained outside and the abdominal wall is pushed out it leads to tremendous negative pressure inside the stomach, it was observed that the pressure inside the stomach becomes -115 mm Hg at the beginning of protrusion of the abdominal wall and when maintained it remains at the level of -55 mm Hg. When the abdomen is pulled inside, intra-gastric pressure reverts to normal. During this practice intra-thoracic pressure becomes markedly positive when abdomen is protruded and near normal when it is retracted.

Thus from the above observations it becomes clear that some of the yogic practices increase the internal pressure while the others decrease it. This pressure variation not only manipulates the internal organs in the mechanical way but also influences its function. Especially the Uddiyana and the Nauli kriya helps in improving the function of digestive tract by mechanical manipulation and also by influencing the circulation of the blood, through the important organs responsible for the digestion.

EFFECTS ON CARDIO VASCULAR SYSTEM

Many of the yogic practices either because of the position in which the body is maintained (e.g. topsy-turvy postures) or because of their influence on internal pressure, ultimately affect the function of the heart and the blood circulation.

FOLLOWING IS THE EXPERIMENTAL OBSERVATIONS :

1 BLOOD PRESSURE CHANGES IN TOPSY-TURVY POSTURES

Studies on eleven subjects during the maintenance of Sarvangasana showed the rise in the systolic blood pressure by 25%. In Shirshasana systolic blood pressure was found to rise by 4% to 10% and diastolic by 14 to 22%. During the five minutes maintenance period the maximum change was seen during the third minute. After reversing the Asana it took one minute for the blood pressure to come back to normal level. Though the blood pressure increases in these two practices; it is much less, when compared to the effect observed in case of weight lifting where systolic blood pressure rises by 63%.

2 EFFECT ON UJJAYI ON CARDIAC OUT PUT :

Cardiac output in Ujjayi Pranayama was found to increase by 17% and heart rate was seen to decrease by 15 beats/min. This Ujjayi breathing had a Puraka phase of 5 sec and Rechaka phase of 10 sec and there was no Kumbhaka phase.

3 EFFECT OF BANDHAS ON PERIPHERAL BLOOD FLOW :
The finger blood flow was measured during different phases of breathing, with and without application of Bandhas in, Yoga-trained as well as untrained subjects. For both the groups it was less in inspiratory phase than in expiratory phase, the value being least in inspiration with the Bandhas and the greatest in deep expiration without the Bandhas. The finger blood flow was less in all cases for untrained subjects than for the trained subjects. This probably indicates the peripheral vasoconstriction which occurs due to increased intra-thoracic pressure during Kumbhaka.

4 EFFECT OF PRANAYAMA ON FINGER TEMPERATURE :
The finger temperature and the finger pulse volume was measured before, during and after the practice of Ujjayi, Kapalabhati and Bhastrika. It was seen that the finger temperature decreased in all the three cases and finger pulse volume decreased in Ujjayi and Bhastrika only. In Kapalabhati the finger pulse showed an increase.

5 EFFECT OF PRANAYAMA ON HEART RATE AND BLOOD PRESSURE :
At the end of the 12-week training in Pranayama alone which consisted of practice of Ujjayi and Kapalabhati done for 15 minutes each, the basal heart rate as well as the basal systolic blood pressure, came down significantly with the simultaneous reduction in the pulse pressure. The double product (heart rate X systolic blood pressure) which indicates the myocardial oxygen consumption also showed a reduction.

6 CARDIOVASCULAR EFFICIENCY
In the maintenance of proper health and physical fitness, Cardiovascular fitness plays a vital role. The 'Haward Step Test', considered as the reliable test for measuring cardiovascular efficiency was used in eleven male students and it indicated that daily one hour session of yogic practices done over the period of 9 months, improves their efficiency significantly.

Thus from the above observations it seems that the long term training in yogic practices would reduce the work load over the heart during basal condition. This finding would be useful in cases where the person is suffering from high blood pressure and over straining of the heart function.

HAEMATALOGICAL AND BIOCHEMICAL CHANGES

Yogic practices, especially Pranayama have been reported to have immediate influence on the blood composition of its various cellular and chemical components.

FOLLOWING ARE THE EXPERIMENTAL OBSERVATIONS :

1 CHANGES DUE TO UJJAYI PRANAYAMA :

In 5 subjects who performed Ujjayi for 25 minutes which included Puraka of 6 sec, Kumbhaka of 12 sec and Rechaka of 12 sec showed a consistent but marginal fall in Hb. by 0.47% and R.B.C. count by 0.14 million-cubic millimetre and a significant fall in packed cell volume (P.C.V.) by 2.86%. This indicates the possibility of Haemodilution which might have occurred because of the shift of fluid from the extra vascular compartment into intra vascular compartment. There was no significant change in any of the biochemical component.

2 EFFECT DUE TO KAPALABHATI :

The same Haemodilution effect as above, was seen in 5 subjects who performed Kapalabhati for 15 minutes. But additionally it also showed a significant change in biochemical parameters. The blood glucose showed a decrease of 3.89 mg per cent, while the free fatty acids showed an increase by 160.55 mg.

3 EFFECT OF LONG TERM TRAINING IN PRANAYAMA :

At the end of 12 weeks training in Pranayama alone, consisting of practice of Ujjayi and Kapalabhati for 15 minutes each; showed a significant increase in W.B.C. count by 9.5 thousand/cubic mm and also a significant fall in free fatty acid levels. The observations confirmed the view that the Pranayamic practices influence the Haematological and biochemical composition only to a small extent. The long term training in Pranayama also helps in reduction of the stress oriented factors as is seen by the reduction in the level of free fatty acids.

4 EFFECT OF YOGA ON CHOLESTEROL LEVEL :

The three weeks of training in Yoga given to 22 males and 10 females showed a significant decrease in the serum level of cholesterol in those cases where it was high. This training also helped in maintaining cholesterol level in normal limit.

5 EFFECT OF YOGA ON SERUM PROTEINS :

The 6 months Yogic training given to 21 patients suffering from Bronchial asthma showed the marked increase in the serum albumin level, a decrease in the serum globulin and no change in tyrosine and total protein fractions. The above two findings have important bearings in the treatment of patients suffering from Bronchial asthma and hypercholesterolaemia through Yogic practices.

6 UROPEPSIN EXCRETION AS INFLUENCED BY ASANAS :

A relationship has been established between the excretion of Uropepsin in the urine, and the adrenal cortical function. Uropepsin excretion in eleven male and eight female subjects was found to reduce significantly at the end of four weeks training in Yoga indicating the tranquillising and relaxing effects of Asanas.

7 UROPEPSIN EXCRETION AS INFLUENCED BY DHAUTIS :

In six male subjects, uropepsin excretion in the urine after the practice of Danda Dhauti and Vastra Dhauti was found to increase, prominently during the first three hours of the practice and more so in the case of Vastra Dhauti. This explains the role played by Dhautis in the treatment of asthma, eczema and other allergic conditions where cortisone therapy plays an effective role and brings forth the importance of Dhautis as a substitute or adjunct to cortisone therapy.

EFFECT ON RESPIRATORY SYSTEM

Number of yogic practices including Pranayama have a significant influence on the functioning of the respiratory system.

FOLLOWING ARE THE EXPERIMENTAL OBSERVATIONS

1 **EFFECT OF YOGA ON VITAL CAPACITY :**
After three weeks training in the yoga given to 24 subjects the vital capacity was found to increase significantly from 3399 ml to 3443 ml.

2 **EFFECT OF YOGA ON PEAK FLOW RATE :**
The peak expiratory flow rate was found to increase significantly at the end of three weeks of training in yoga given to 105 females.

3 **EFFECT OF PRANAYAMA ON THE MINUTE VENTILATION AND GAS EXCHANGE :**
As seen in 10 subjects, minute ventilation was 4.8 Lt. during Ujjayi Pranayama as compared to 8.9 Lt. during normal breathing. During Kapalabhati it increases to 31.2 Lt. The alveolar and the blood gas composition did not show any significant change even after the performance of Ujjayi for 15 minutes. After the performance of Kapalabhati for 15 minutes the alveolar and blood gas composition showed reduction in CO2 level and consequent increase in Oxygen level. The blood pH showed a mild increase. Thus it seems, though the minute ventilation is significantly reduced in Ujjayi there is no significant change in alveolar or blood gas composition because the effective alveolar ventilation remain more or less same. On the other hand during Kapalabhati the increase in the minute ventilation leads to a slight reduction in the alveolar CO2 but this is not sufficient to increase the blood pH to that level which would cause respiratory alkalosis.

4 **EFFECT OF KAPALABHATI ON BREATH HOLDING TIME :**
The ability to hold the breath inside, was found to increase from the average of 37 sec before, to 54 sec after the Kapalabhati was performed for one minute.

5 EFFECT OF BANDHAS ON BREATH HOLDING TIME :
The application of Bandhas during the Kumbhaka phase have been found to increase the breath holding time from 20.3 sec to 47.3 sec. Thus the Bandhas seems to have an important role in the Kumbhaka phase of Pranayama.

6 EFFECT OF BRAHMAMUDRA ON LUNG VENTILATION:
Turning the head towards the right or left side as done in Brahmamudra leads to increase in the transparence of lung fields on the side towards which the head was turned when observed under fluoroscopy. It indicates the increased ventilation in that area. Similarly in Chakrasana the ventilation of the lung especially in the apical area on the opposite side of the bend has been found to increase.

The above observations indicate how the various yogic practices improve the ventilation, but without causing any marked disturbance in the functioning of the respiratory system as far as the gaseous exchange is concerned. Essentially the manipulation of breathing pattern in Pranayama seems to cause minimal disturbance in any of the homoeostatic mechanism but nonetheless markedly affects the functioning of various system as described in the subsequent part of this review.

EFFECT ON DIGESTIVE SYSTEM AND METABOLISM

Some of the kriyas like Dhauti, Basti and Nauli influence the functioning of the digestive system significantly. The energy metabolism is also influenced by various yogic practices.

1 EFFECT OF DANDA DHAUTI AND VASTRA DHAUTI ON GASTRIC ACIDITY :
Eleven subjects practising Danda Dhauti and three subjects practising Vastra Dhauti were examined. The results indicated that with the practice of both the Dhautis, hyper-acidity was significantly reduced while achlorohydric subjects had a better secretion of free

acid. Danda Dhauti particularly seems to reduce acidity for about one hour after the practice. Combined acid was observed to be increased by Danda Dhauti while free acid was decreased.

2 **EFFECT OF AIR SWALLOWING ON THE GASTRIC ACIDITY :**
In three subjects who had hyper-acidity showed a decrease in the free, combined and total acidity after Vayu Bhakshana (air swallowing) for a period of one hour.

3 **EFFECT OF MEDITATION ON ENERGY EXPENDITURE :**
During the session of meditation spread over 45 minutes, the energy expenditure showed a significant progressive reduction from 37 cal/sq M./Hr. in resting sitting position to 29.7cal/sq M./Hr.

4 **EFFECT OF YOGA ON BASAL METABOLIC RATE :**
By the 10 weeks training in Yoga in 20 subjects the Basal Metabolic rate was seen to decrease by 12.8%.

The above observation concerning the effect of Kriyas on the gastric function have an important clinical application in the patients suffering from hyper-acidity. Apart from the Kriyas, Yoga as a whole helps in reducing the stress response making a person more relaxed as seen by the changes in the level of energy expenditure.

EFFECT ON NERVOUS SYSTEM AND PSYCHO-MOTOR FUNCTIONS

The most important effects of the Yogic practices are found to be on the nervous system as well as on the behavioural pattern.

FOLLOWING ARE THE EXPERIMENTAL OBSERVATIONS:

1 **EFFECT OF YOGA ON AUTONOMIC NERVOUS SYSTEM :**
After the two months training in Yoga in 44 high school boys the functioning of the autonomic nervous system showed the shift towards the increased para-sympathetic activity.

2 **EFFECT OF YOGA ON PSYCHO MOTOR PERFORMANCE :**
Speed, accuracy and coordination was found to improve significantly when tested, employing 'Tweezer Dexterity Test' in 35 subjects at the end of 3 weeks of training in Yoga.

3 **EFFECT OF YOGA ON MENTAL FATIGUE :**
At the end of 3 weeks of training in Yoga in 32 subjects, the overall performance of the mental work was found to improve significantly.

4 **EFFECT OF YOGA ON IMMEDIATE MEMORY :**
At the end of 3 weeks of training in Yoga, in 73 subjects the immediate memory was found to show marked improvement.

5 **EFFECT OF YOGA ON ANXIETY LEVEL :**
At the end of 3 weeks of training in Yoga in 56 subjects, the score of the total anxiety level was found to reduce significantly.

6 **EFFECT OF DIFFERENT PITCH OF 'OMKARA' RECITATION ON PSYCHO-MOTOR PERFORMANCE :**
Ten subjects were made to recite 10 Omkar in low as well as in high pitch and their psycho-motor performance was observed. The performance reduced after the low pitch recitation, showing the influence of low pitch omkar recitation making the mind more introverted.

7 **MENTAL FATIGUE AS INFLUENCED BY PRANAYAMA :**
In 30 subjects practise of Ujjayi Pranayama was observed to delay the onset of mental fatigue in performing the mathematical calculation and helped subjects to improve their mental efficiency.

8 **EFFECT OF PRANAYAMA ON EEG. :**
All the three practices of Ujjayi, Kapalabhati and Bhastrika produce increased synchronisation of EEG., in an awake phase, as indicated by higher amplitude and longer period of Alpha burst. These change concur with the subjective report of feeling of mental quietude and reduction in distraction due to thought process.

EXTRAORDINARY CONTROL OVER THE BODY FUNCTIONS

The long term practice of yoga, as seen in some Yogis, enables them to exercise control over some of the involuntary functions of the body viz. activity of the heart, circulation, metabolism.

FOLLOWING ARE THE EXPERIMENTAL OBSERVATIONS

1 CONTROL OF HEART RATE :

When the activity of the heart was studied in one subject with the help of ECG., it was observed that he could slow down his heart rate tremendously leading to stoppage of the heart for 3.02 to 5.6 sec on six different occasions. To induce this effect he used to apply Uddiyana and Jalandhar Bandha during internal retention of breath. X-ray examination revealed slight dilation of heart during this period. Apart from this experimental observations, there are also some studies in which some subjects could slow down the heart to about 30 to 35 beats/min as compared to normal rate or 72/min.

2 UNDERGROUND BURIAL OR 'BHUGARBHA SAMADHI' :

In one experiment it was observed that during his stay in an air tight box, the oxygen requirement in one Yogi was found to be reduced by 50% as compared to his oxygen needs under basal condition. The subject experienced no inconvenience even when the oxygen content of air tight box was about 14% and carbon dioxide 5%. In another experiment of the similar type it was observed that the training in Pranayama helped the individual to develop the capacity to withstand the stress produced by high CO_2 which sometimes goes upto 7.6% in the air tight space.

3 CONTROL OF TEMPERATURE OF THE PALMS :

In one Yogi it was observed that he could produce the temperature difference of 10 C. between the two regions of the same palm when the temperature was monitored with the help of thermistors. The Thenar eminence part of the palm showed fall in the temperature while in Hypothenar area it increased. To bring out this effect a particular Pranayamic technique was practised by that Yogi.

4 DOMINANCE OF ONE NOSTRIL AND EFFECT OF YOGA-DANDA ON IT :

In one set of experiment it was observed that out of 96 subjects 47.8% showed dominance of right nostril, 37.7% of left nostril while only 14.5% had equal activity in both the nostrils. By placing the Yoga-danda under the arm-pit it was observed that within two minutes the opposite nostril opens up fully and the nostril on the same side starts working less than before. In another set of experiment, the cyclical change in the nasal resistance was observed in two subjects and was found to have a consistent regular pattern over a period of 24 hours.

Thus from the above observations it seems that some of the individuals develop an ability to control, autonomic functions through the long-term practice of Yoga

NOTE :

In the above review we have given only the gist of conclusions of some of the important investigations carried out at Kaivalyadhama, Lonavla as well as in other centres all over the world. For more detailed information please refer (1) 'Abstracts and Bibliography of Articles on Yoga', published by Kaivalyadhama, Lonavla; and (2) 'Science Studies Yoga', published by Himalayan International Institute of Yoga Science and Philosophy, Philadelphia, U.S.A.

PART IV

GLOSSARY OF THE IMPORTANT WORDS

GLOSSARY OF THE IMPORTANT WORDS

AJNA CHAKRA : Energy centre along the Sushumna at the level of eyebrows in the centre of the head.

ANABOLISM : The process concerned with conversion of the food for building up of the body tissues.

ANAHATA CHAKRA : Energy centre along the Sushumna at the level of the heart in the chest region.

ANANDAMAYA KOSH : Subtlest of the Koshas in which one has an experience of an unqualified, pure blissful consciousness.

ANNAMAYA KOSHA : Most gross of the Koshas, made up of and sustained by the food-level of physical existence.

ANTAGONISTS : Muscles which act in opposite way to that of the prime movers.

APANA : That aspect of the Pranashakti which is concerned with the removal of the waste matter out of the body.

AUTONOMIC NERVOUS SYSTEM : That functional part of the nervous system which is concerned with the regulation of visceral organs.

BIOFEEDBACK TECHNIQUE : A process through which one can become aware of the internal functions by converting it into auditory or visual signal and where by one can learn to modify them.

CALCIFICATION: A process of deposition of calcium in the bone which is responsible for the hardness of the healthy bone.

CATABOLISM : The process concerned with the breakdown of the food and its conversion into energy.

CELL : Smallest structural unit of the body that can have independent life.

CHAKRA : Energy centres along the Sushumna Nadi.

CIRCADIAN RHYTHM : A cyclical biological change in internal functions occurring with a rough frequency of twenty for hours.

CONSCIOUSNESS : A state of being aware of oneself as distinct and separate entity in relation to one's environment.

DIASTOLE : Relaxation of heart muscles especially when the blood enters inside the ventricles.

ECG- ELECTROCARDIOGRAM : Record of the electrical activity of the heart.

EEG- ELECTROENCEPHALOGRAM : Record of the electrical activity of the brain.

EMG - ELECTROMYOGRAM : Record of the electrical activity of the muscle.

ENTEROCEPTION : The process of detecting changes taking place inside the body. It is made up of proprioception and visceroception.

EXTENSION : Movement in the joint where the flexion is reversed.

EXTEROCEPTION : The process of detecting changes taking place outside the body.

FLEXION : Bending of the body part where the angle in the joint diminishes.

FIXATORS : Muscles which assist the prime movers by fixing the various parts of the body.

GLOTTIS : The opening between the vocal cords.

HOMOEOSTASIS : A complex process through which internal functions of the body are maintained in a dynamically balanced state.

HYPERMETABOLIC STATE : A state of increased metabolic activity as in case of reaction to the Stress.

HYPERTENSION : Abnormally high blood pressure.

HYPOMETABOLIC STATE : A state of reduced metabolic activities as in case of Meditative state of Yoga.

IDA NADI : The Nadi starting from the base of the spine of LEFT side and reaching the LEFT nostril.

INTERSTITIAL FLUID : Body fluid outside the blood vessels surrounding the cells part of which gets collected in lymphatic vessels and is also known as Lymph.

ISOMETRIC CONTRACTION : It is a type of contraction when the muscle tension increases without any apparent shortening of its length.

ISOTONIC CONTRACTION : It is a type of contraction wherein the muscle shorten in length against the constant resistance.

KOSHA : Concept of hierarchical existence and operation of human organism at various levels, simultaneously.

KUNDALINI : Spiritual energy which remains dormant at the base of the spine and when activated reaches the highest centre in the head.

KYPHOSIS : Increases curvature of the spine mainly in the dorsal region with convexity backward.

LARYNX : Voice box situated in the neck below the throat and above the trachea, which contains the vocal cords.

LORDOSIS : Increased curvature of the spine in the cervical or Lumbar region with the convexity forward.

LYMPH : The fluid oozed out from the capillaries which after coming in contact with the cells return to the heart through the lymphatics.

MANIPURA CHAKRA : Energy centre along the Sushumna at the level of umbilicus inside the abdomen.

MANOMAYA KOSHA : Existence and operation at the level of mental functioning viz. Emotion and Memory.

METABOLISM : The process of assimilation of food and its use for the growth, tissue repair and the elimination of waste matter. It is a sum total of anabolism and catabolism.

MULADHARA CHAKRA : Energy centre at the base of the spine along the perineum where the Kundalini is said to remain in dormant state.

MYOCARDIAL ISCHAEMIA : The condition where blood supply to the myocardial cells is reduced due to spasm or the occlusion of the coronary vessels.

MYOCARDIAL INFARCTION : The condition wherein the myocardial cells get damaged due to sudden blockage of the coronary vessels by the free-floating blood clot inside the blood stream.

MYOFIBRILS : Elongated fibre like muscle cells, when grouped into bundles form the muscle mass.

NADI : Passage for the movement of the Pranashakti, inside the body.

ORGAN : A structure in a body where various tissues come together to serve some specific function.

OSTEOPOROSIS : A process of reduction in the density of the bone due to removal of calcium from it leading to brittleness of the bone.

PARASYMPATHETIC NERVOUS SYSTEM : Part of the autonomic nervous system that is concerned with the control of the 'resting' functions of body.

PERINEUM : Part of the pelvic floor, between the genitals in the front and anus behind.

PHARYNX : Area also known as throat, forms the part of the air passage between the nasal cavity and the larynx, as well as acts as a conduit for the food from the oral cavity to the oesophagus.

PINGALA NADI : The nadi which starts from the base of the spine on the RIGHT side and reaches the RIGHT nostril.

POSTURE : Arrangement of the body part for the purpose of maintaining stationary position or the moving actions of the body.

PRANA : The bio-energy which enlivens the human body and is responsible for all its psycho-physiological actions.

PRANAMAYA KOSHA : Existence at the level of physiological functions.

PRIME MOVERS : Muscles, primarily responsible for the particular movement.

PROPRIOCEPTIVE SENSATION : The sensation for determining the position and movements of the body and limbs.

PSYCHO-SOMATIC : An inter-relationship between the body and mind where physical actions are affected by the mental condition and vice versa.

SAHASRARA CHAKRA : Highest energy centre situated inside the head. When the Kundalini reaches this centre, one experiences a transcendental consciousness.

SAMANA : That aspect of the Pranashakti which is responsible for the conversion of external source of energy into a assimilable form.

SCOLIOSIS : Abnormal sideward bend in the spinal column.

SUSHUMNA NADI : The Nadi which runs along the spinal column, between Ida and Pingla Nadi and reaches Sahasrara Chakra in the Head.

SYNERGIST : Muscles which assist prime movers by contracting simultaneously during particular movement.

SYMPATHETIC NERVOUS SYSTEM : That part of the autonomic nervous system which is concerned with the 'aroused' state of the body functions.

SYSTEM : Grouping of various organs to serve some specific generalised functions of the body.

SWADHISTHANA CHAKRA : Energy centre along the Sushumna at the level of pubic syphysis just above the genitals.

TISSUE : Grouping of cells having similar structures.

TONE : Tightness in the resting muscle due to minimal contraction of the few muscle fibres.

TURIA : Transcendental state of consciousness.

UDANA : That aspect of Pranashakti which is concerned with thinking and its expression.

VARICOSITY : Dilation of the veins due to damage to its wall and the internal valves, leading to inefficient venous return.

VIJANANAMAYA KOSHA : Existence and operation at the level of Intelligence.

VISCERA : All the organs inside the abdomen and thorax.

VISCEROCEPTIVE SENSATION : A process through which one can get information regarding the visceral functions.

VISHUDDHA CHAKRA : Energy centre along the Sushumna at the level of larynx inside the neck.

VOCAL CORDS : Horizontal folds of mucus membrane with some muscle tissue in it, in the larynx which are responsible for the production of voice.

VYANA : That aspect of Pranashakti which is responsible for circulating the assimilated energy all over the body.

* * * *

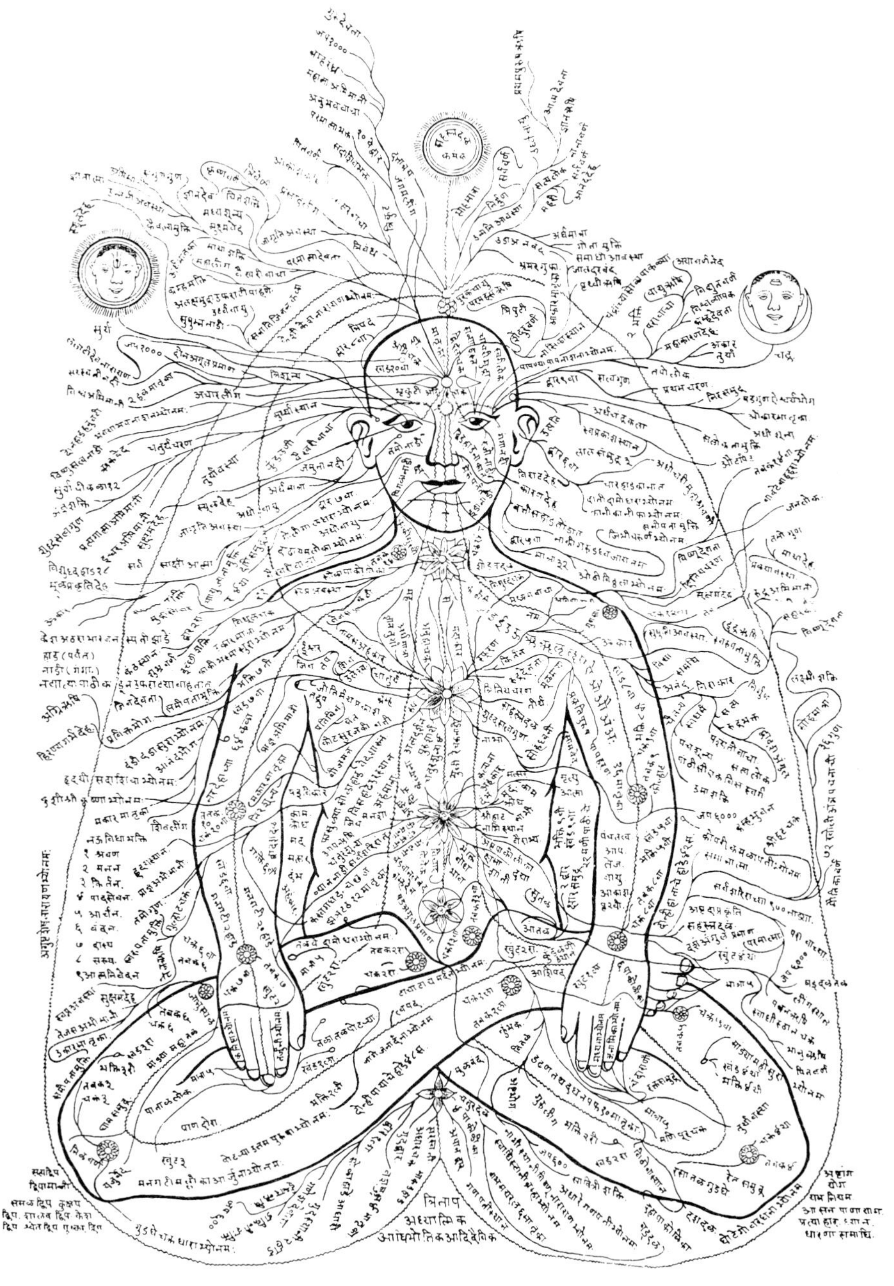
त्रिताप
अध्यात्मिक